Your performance the other night gave me such rare pleasure that I asked the organiser if he had flown you all in specially for the occasion from some far-off enchanted region.

Laurie Lee

Published by Little Toller Books in 2024
Ford, Pineapple Lane, Dorset

Words, music and lyrics © Jehanne Mehta 2024
Foreword © Jonathon Porritt 2024
Introduction, Afterword © Jojo Mehta 2024

The author asserts her moral right to be identified as the author of her works in accordance with the Copyright, Design and Patents Act 1988

Illustration © Stu McLellan 2024

Typeset by Little Toller Books

Printed in Sussex by Pureprint

All papers used by Little Toller Books are natural, recyclable products made from wood grown in sustainable, well-managed forests

A catalogue record for this book is available from the British Library

All rights reserved

ISBN 978-1-915068-39-2

Earth Songs

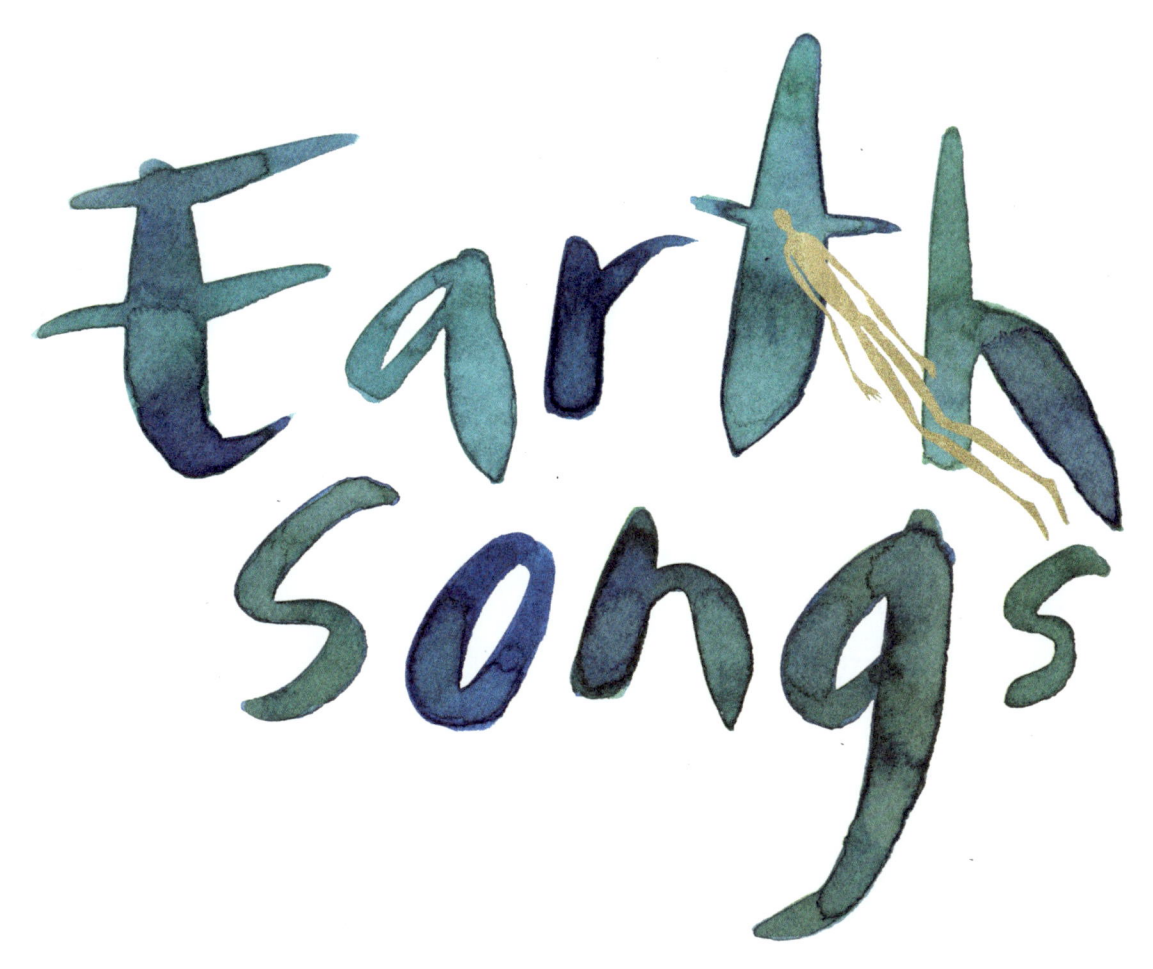

JEHANNE MEHTA

Illustrated by

STU MCLELLAN

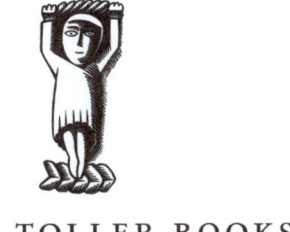

LITTLE TOLLER BOOKS

Her songs are highly original and very singable, and why more people don't perform them is beyond us. If ever a song-maker deserved to be better known, it's Jehanne.

Fo'c'sle News

Contents

Foreword *Jonathon Porritt* — 7
Introduction *Jojo Mehta* — 9
Biography — 11
Songwriting *Jehanne Mehta* — 13

Seasons

New Year — 16
House of Snow — 18
February — 20
New Season of the Spring — 22
April Fool — 24
Green Jack — 26
Herb Song — 28
June Morning — 30
The Smell of New Hay — 32
The Corn King — 34
Harvest Festival — 36
Shooting Stars — 38
Autumn into Winter — 40
Winter Solstice — 42
Bells at Midnight — 44

Activism

People of the Earth — 48
Blue Whale — 52
This Power — 54
Lament for the Trees — 56
Bobbin of Yarn — 60
Make my Peace — 64
Stop the World — 68
Emblem — 70
Lord in the Green — 72

Soul's Journey

Humming Top	78
Love is a Song	80
Corridors of Time	82
Je Me Pardonne	84
Pathway with a Heart	86
Pipy's Song	88
That Fire	90
I Did Not Leave	92

Albion

This Place	96
Song of the Fosterer	98
Song Hunt	102
The Slow Motion Waltz	104
River Man	106
The Rollright Stones	108
Edward	110
The Fields of Runnymede	112
The Greenway	114
The Metal Worker's Apprentice	116

Myth and Legend

Arthur the King	122
La Belle Dormant	124
The Fountain	126
Basket of Roses	128
The Bunch of Keys	130
Jean Soleil	132
The Three Sillies	134
The Juggler	136

Afterword *Jojo Mehta* — 139
Acknowledgements — 141
Our Mother — 143

Foreword
Jonathon Porritt

I lived with Jehanne Mehta (or Sylvia, as she was then) back in the 1980s. Not literally (otherwise her lifetime partner Rob might have been a bit concerned!), but through her work. I bought three of her cassettes at that time (only one of which, *Green Jack*, still survives), and they got a lot of airtime.

No one was more surprised to hear this than Jojo when she asked me, somewhat out of the blue, to write this Foreword. I've been playing *Green Jack* ever since!

I live most of the time in my head. I've always been a words-person, left-hemisphere, crunching numbers, endlessly analysing and intellectualising. When I joined the Ecology Party in the mid-70s, 'green politics' was very much in its infancy. 'The environment' was seen as something out there, polluted and assaulted by destructive economic development, and it was our job to protect it and make sure it was used on a much more sustainable basis. It was all very transactional.

Happily, my early encounters with inspirational voices in the Deep Ecology and Ecofeminism movements (with Jehanne playing away in the background) rescued me from what could easily have become an arid, denatured world of sad eco-wonks!

Head and heart. I sometimes wonder if one of the reasons why we've made so little progress (relatively speaking) in addressing today's nature and climate crises is because the Environment Movement has always been more head than heart. We've yearned so strenuously for scientific credibility, for impregnable rationality beyond the reach of soul-destroying media contempt, that we've sometimes forgotten to keep on telling the single most important story we have about who we are as a species.

Just as I was sitting down to write this Foreword, and celebrating my rediscovery of Jehanne's direct, evocative lyrics, a new campaign was launched (WE ARE NATURE) with a deceptively simple objective of getting every dictionary (including the Oxford English Dictionary) to change its definition of Nature. At the moment, those definitions talk about the rest of life on earth *excluding* humankind. What the campaign hopes to achieve is to ensure that all future definitions *include* humankind in our understanding of Nature.

Sorry if I keep harking back to the 1980s (as you'll see in this wonderfully inspiring selection of her songs, Jehanne's work has spanned all the decades since then), but there's something special in formative influences – one of whom, for me, was a US-based philosopher called Willis Harman.

He attributed the emerging crisis (already hiding in plain sight in those days) to what he called 'the ontological assumption of separateness'. I'm no philosopher, so I wrestled with the idea that some assumption of humankind's standing apart from Nature, not being embedded in Nature, went to the heart of the crisis – to the very notion of who we are in our deepest being. Yet is this not still the truth of it? Even now, after 50 years of waging war on Nature to satisfy our own needs and apparently insatiable demands?

Which puts the highest possible value on those who help others overcome that assumption of separateness, who support us as we find our own ways of becoming more embedded in Nature – through their words, their values, their music. Thank you, Jehanne.

Introduction
Jojo Mehta

My mother Jehanne's music was the soundtrack to my childhood. I knew all the lyrics of her early albums by heart. But it wasn't until I reached my thirties and had done some literal and musical travelling that I realised what a darn good songwriter she was. I discovered it's not so common to find satisfying and singable melodies with clear yet poetic lyrics that can speak equally to emotional, ecological and mythological topics without preaching, protest or pretension.

Her writing has a heartfelt yet unsentimental quality that allows her songs to speak directly and movingly to an audience. I have attended many of her performances over the years (I should really say 'their' performances, as while the writing may have been hers, the playing and harmonies were always with my father) and have come to fully expect tears glistening on cheeks as I look around the room.

Socially quite shy, politically and spiritually radical, and deeply thoughtful, Jehanne is a true creative: she writes because she has to. She always described a song as if it had its own independent being. I remember she never used to say 'I'm writing a song'. Instead she would say 'a song is coming'. She didn't chase fame or fortune, but quietly asserted that the songs had their own life and needed to 'go out into the world'. She was always delighted to hear that someone from a far-off country had discovered her recordings, or that someone had 'grown up' with her songs.

She occasionally wrote on commission, and if she did, this involved experiential research (an example is *The Metal Worker's Apprentice*); but even then she would only start to write, as she always did, when a song 'wanted to come'. Inspiration was always sparked by a deeply felt connection: to a person, to an understanding, to a story that held meaning for her, and most of all to the Earth, often in the form of a particular place at a particular time or season. The cycle of the year and its echoes in the psyche were a rich resource, as were the myths and legends of the English landscapes she deeply inhabits. When I say deeply, I mean that her connection to the land feels profoundly rooted and many-dimensional, in a way that I can only describe as indigenous.

At the time of publication, my mother is 83. She performs only rarely these days, for local occasions. She has written well over 150 songs, of which around 90 have been recorded. They are a joy to sing, and they deserve to be sung, which is why this book is in your hands. The lyrics are also tuneful poems that are a joy to read, and they deserve to be beautifully brought to life on the page, which is how this book has come to be.

 Jehanne cares deeply – about life, about love, about legend and above all about the living world – and that is what these songs capture. We recognise in them our own deep care and desire for connection to all those things, and to each other.

 They are her legacy, and they are also seeds, to be lovingly scattered.

Photo by Sylvain Guenot

Biography

Jehanne Mehta (née Sylvia Mathews in 1941) first started playing guitar at the age of 15 and bought her own Spanish guitar at the age of 17. Having taken a few lessons in flamenco guitar, she fell in love with folk music while a Modern Languages student at Keele University, where she sang in a student folk band, The Keele Row with Dick Barton, Geoff Iliffe and Rob Mehta (whom she married in 1965 when she was 24 and he 23).

Together they ran the university folk club which was host to the early gigs of some major names such as Bert Jansch (who slept on Rob's floor) and the young Martin Carthy. Carthy was a huge inspiration to Sylvia (as she was then known): listening to him she knew she had found the kind of music she wanted to sing. The Keele Row sang in folk clubs in Birmingham, Manchester, Liverpool and London (The Troubadour).

The story of her work from that time on is also the story of both a musical and life-long partnership with husband Rob. Both trained and worked as teachers but they played regular spots together at local folk clubs and other venues in Oxfordshire, she singing with guitar, accompanied by Rob on the fiddle or mandolin. After the birth of their first child in 1967 she wrote her first song.

Whilst Rob continued performing (with Banbury group The Poachers) during the 1970s, when she would occasionally join him for a gig, it was not until they moved to Gloucestershire in 1979 with their three children (then twelve, seven and five) that her songwriting became more of a dedicated focus and they began to find opportunities to play her original material.

Jehanne's most prolific period came in the 1980s when she developed some of the interweaving themes which were to emerge strongly over the rest of her songwriting career: myth and legend, especially of place; the turning of the seasons; the inner journey of the soul; and a committed activism for nature. Jehanne and Rob played under the name Green Jack and recorded four albums, three of which are still available. Session musicians John Ralph and Bron Bradshaw joined them, as did Ric Sanders and Chris Leslie, both to become well-known members of iconic folk collective Fairport Convention. (Chris, who plays on all of the 1980s recordings, took his first fiddle lessons from Rob in rural Oxfordshire, quickly revealed a prodigious teenage talent, clearly destined for the instrument.)

Jehanne also began writing songs in French at this time. She had felt a strong connection with the language since an extended French stay in her late teens (in a household with a large world music collection) as well as with certain areas of France. She felt a particular affinity with the area sometimes termed 'Cathar country' after the radical Christian sect that flourished in the south of France in the 12th and 13th centuries, an egalitarian and highly cultured group that allowed women to become initiates. This connection was strong enough to inspire an official name change to Jehanne, which is the old French version of Jean/Joan, and the description of her as a 'troubadour' (the travelling court lyric poets and musicians of that time) has been echoed from several quarters. Jehanne recalls she felt 'immediately more at home in herself' with this name. Jehanne and Rob visited France most years in the 1980s and early 1990s.

In the early 1990s came a new phase when a third musician expanded their usual duo to a trio. This was Will Mercer, an exceptionally versatile guitarist, bass and mandolin player with whom they toured, performed and recorded for the next 25+ years under the name Earthwards. A major European tour in 1993 was a test of whether touring was the life they wanted to lead. It exhausted Jehanne and took a considerable toll on her health. They decided to remain based in the Cotswold market town of Stroud with occasional shorter European tours (especially in Ireland, the Netherlands, France and Germany), and over many years continued to grow a small but dedicated international following. Recordings of Jehanne's songs have reached Australia, China, Croatia, France, Germany, Ireland, Latin America, the Netherlands, Russia, Spain, Switzerland, Türkiye and the US. Many children have been brought up listening to them.

Earthwards recorded three further albums. *Rose in Deep Water* (1992) exemplifies Jehanne's mature style, with tracks combining folk, chanson, Spanish and jazz influences in a unique mix all her own. The much later *Emblem* (2006) and *This Place* (2015) signal more of a return to her folk roots and include tracks written many years before but never recorded. The themes she evolved during the 1980s, however, remain alive throughout.

Songwriting
Jehanne Mehta

These songs have been written over a period of fifty-five years. It was the enjoyment of listening to and singing traditional British folk songs which made me want to write songs myself. The British tradition is a cornucopia of riches which I feel stretches back in mood, and also in some content, to Celtic times. Some of these songs are closer to the traditional mood than others. It would take lifetimes to learn all there is to be learnt from our tradition.

The songs do not belong to me, although I feel responsible for how they get on in the world. When I first started to write them the process was very much an inspirational one. I often did not know what I was going to write about (see *Song Hunt*). Form and content came from somewhere with little work on my part, sometimes very quickly, and sometimes lyrics and melody both at once. Later a theme might be decided on beforehand, but I had to wait, sometimes a long time, for the creative moment when the tune suddenly began to arrive, or the words, or both. Once this started to happen, I had to orientate my mind to the theme, and felt driven until I'd done the work of creating, shaping and cutting. Once a song was finished, I was often surprised at what had been written and often found I had learnt a lot on several levels from the creative effort involved.

It remains to point out the obvious. A song is hardly complete without the melody, although some of the lyrics may stand on their own. The purpose of this song book, however, is to enable you to sing them yourselves. If, in singing these songs and pondering on them, you might recognise some of your own experiences reflected back to you and can feel your heart warmed by them, then I shall feel I have gone a little way towards achieving what song, and in particular folk song, has done for me.

For Jehanne's recordings and to listen to samples of many of the songs in this book, please visit ***www.jehannemehta.com***

Jehanne is a lovely songwriter. She writes from the heart ... her songs give a sense of reflecting on important things to do with nature, to do with ecology, to do with our own relationship with all the things that are around us. And there's also a sense of fun and joy in her work. She connects very strongly with cultural depth ... the interconnectivity of us with everything.

Chris Leslie, Fairport Convention

Seasons

New Year

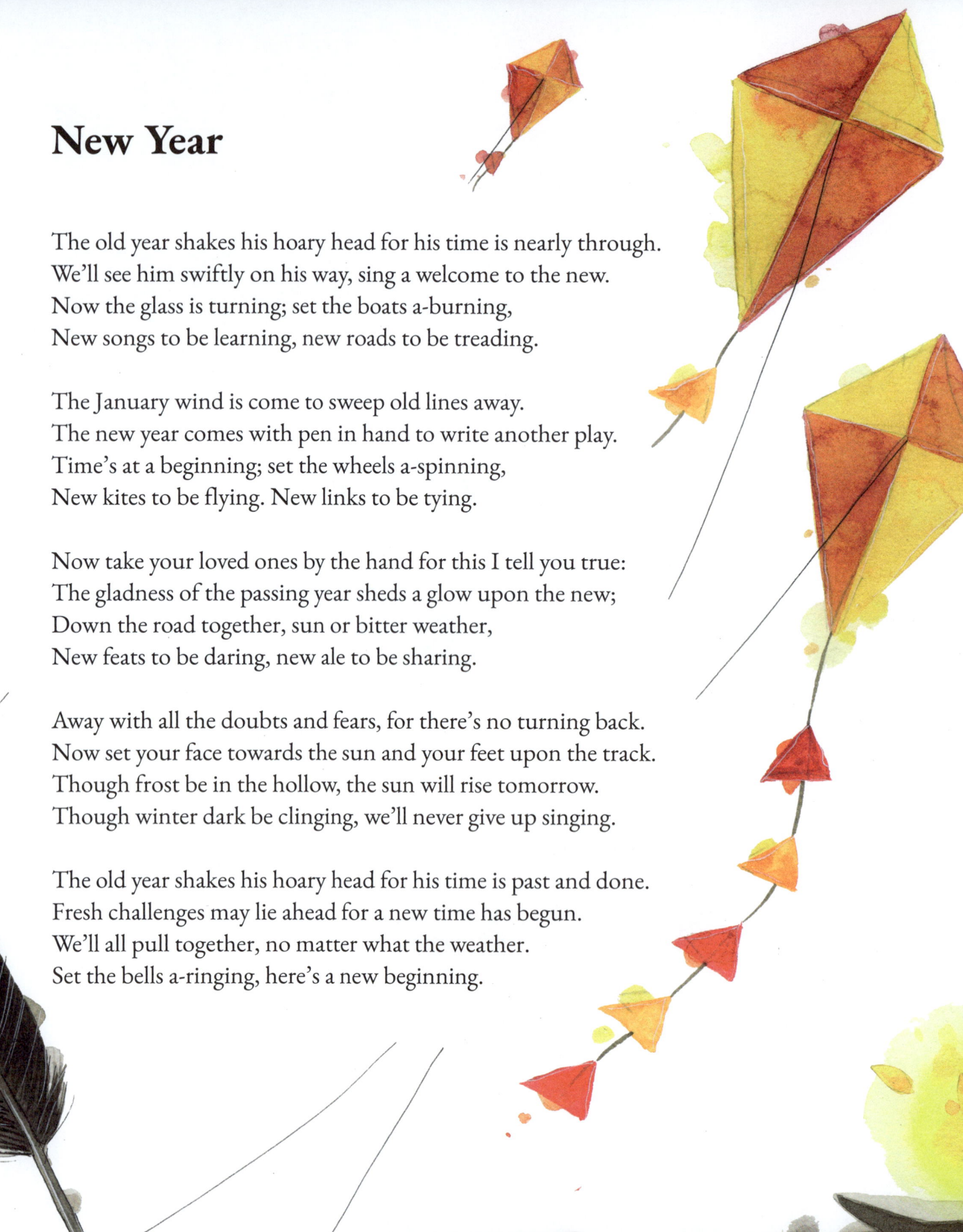

The old year shakes his hoary head for his time is nearly through.
We'll see him swiftly on his way, sing a welcome to the new.
Now the glass is turning; set the boats a-burning,
New songs to be learning, new roads to be treading.

The January wind is come to sweep old lines away.
The new year comes with pen in hand to write another play.
Time's at a beginning; set the wheels a-spinning,
New kites to be flying. New links to be tying.

Now take your loved ones by the hand for this I tell you true:
The gladness of the passing year sheds a glow upon the new;
Down the road together, sun or bitter weather,
New feats to be daring, new ale to be sharing.

Away with all the doubts and fears, for there's no turning back.
Now set your face towards the sun and your feet upon the track.
Though frost be in the hollow, the sun will rise tomorrow.
Though winter dark be clinging, we'll never give up singing.

The old year shakes his hoary head for his time is past and done.
Fresh challenges may lie ahead for a new time has begun.
We'll all pull together, no matter what the weather.
Set the bells a-ringing, here's a new beginning.

House of Snow

The storms have loosened half the slates, the water's dripping in;
There's no refuge from the weather here inside.
There are cracks in every window pane, the green is flooding in
And I could not keep you out, love, if I tried.

For the house of snow is derelict
The frosty flowers have all been picked
The ice has almost melted
And the winter's nearly gone.

The frost has cracked the mortar and the walls are crumbling down;
Brown Jenny's built her nest between the stones.
Under the peeling plaster, the ancient pitted rafter,
The thaw has stripped this dwelling to the bones. *Chorus*

There's a subterranean river rising underneath the floor:
I can feel it in my fingers and my toes
And a shaft of hazy sunlight pierces through the broken door;
You forget about the sunlight when it snows. *Chorus*

There are new leaves in my garden, new traffic on the road;
There is morning light and lark song in your hair.
I shall have to give up shaping new methods of escaping –
When I open up I know you will be there. *Chorus*

There's a kind of easy laughter when you're giving up a fight
And peace is breaking in through every wall,
And nothing more is left you, not a shred or two of pride
And I wonder why I ever fought at all.

Now my house of snow is derelict.
The frosty flowers have all been picked.
I'm coming out to meet you
And the spring is on its way.

February

'February fill the dykes',
That's what the old rhymes call her,
When the tumbling torrents split their sides
And there's mud beside the river,
When thrushes on the rooftops sing
A tantalising ode to spring,
But the east wind hasn't lost its sting
And the winter's not yet over.

O Candlemas if thou be fine,
Spring will be long a-coming,
But if thou bring us clouds and rain,
Why then it's time for roving,
Where the February maids are seen
In bridal white all trimmed with green
And the east wind sweeps the pavements clean
All of a Sunday morning.

It's time to clear the ditches out
And lay the blackthorn hedges.
I'll send my love a valentine
And all my heart's true pledges.
We'll meet beneath the old yew tree
Just long enough to say 'Goodbye'.
Tomorrow I'll be on my way
As far as this road reaches.

It's February clear the decks,
Let every land be shriven.
If we sweep our debris from the sky
The earth will be forgiven.
There's many a carnival played out
On the February roundabout,
And many a beast with horns and snout
Out of his corner driven.

I'll take my music on my back,
I'll take my scarf and jacket
And I'll follow that old March hare along
Through all the toil and traffic.
I'll not expect the year to bring
A fortune fair nor anything
But love and just a chance to sing
These few songs in my pocket.
I'll not expect the year to bring
A fortune fair nor anything
But love and just a chance to sing
The new songs in my pocket.

New Season of the Spring

On morning banks where primroses their gentle warmth have spread
And daisies their white sunrays dip in pools of dawning red,
Where grass is sweet with dew, with dew, the dreams the stars have shed,
I will tune myself as ear for thee, my Lady,
As ear for the new season of the spring.

Where blackbird in the cherry bloom pipes his woodland flute,
Where bullfinch in the thicket chimes his only sweet sad note,
Where robin on the hazel twig opens his crystal throat,
I will be open throat, be voice for thee, my Lady,
Be voice for the new season of the spring.

In streams where trout and minnow hang, poised against the race,
In pools where the grey heron stoops and walks a measured pace,
In springs where flowers all in gold lift up their shining face,
I will dip my hands for words for thee, my Lady,
For words for the new season of the spring.

For everything is changed now and is changing.
The hard dry bone is splintered like old wood.
In waves the new life floods and weaves across the hills and plains.
It is resounding in the water and the blood.

Where rock has stood unchangingly in cliff and cleft and scar,
Where iron, copper, tin and gold the hidden treasures are,
Where ancient stones in circles stood under sun and moon and star,
We will sing abroad the news of thee, my Lady,
The news of the new season of the spring.

April Fool

When I woke up this morning there were rabbits running round my bed,
A fluffy feeling behind my eyes: white rabbits inside my head.
When I came down to breakfast a buck hare was chasing the cat.
When I put on my coat to go outside, oh lord, there was rabbits inside my hat.

There are things that I can see when I am tumbling around
They never taught me when I went to school,
And things that I can hear beside the ringing in my ears,
'Cos I'm an April fool, oh yes, 'cos I'm an April fool.

I tell you there's no end to the ringing, because that's how the fooling goes.
I've got bells on my sceptre and bells in my ears, and bells on the end of my toes.
I'll let you into a confidential secret: I'm really a king in disguise,
Or a queen or a tramp or old Mrs Jones, who smiles when the sun's in her eyes. *Chorus*

Sometimes I get the impression that the world is laughing at me,
But can I help it if standing on my head is the only way that I can see?
This morning I had a mighty row with myself, but what can a poor fellow do
When half of my face is black and half white? I feel as if I'm split in two. *Chorus*

One day as I was a-tumbling, I saw them felling trees all day
And stoking up the engine of this monster machine mowing down the poor folks in its way.
And I met a strange man in dark glasses, but they weren't meant to keep out the sun;
His intent was to lock us all up in our heads 'til all chances for changing were gone. *Chorus*

Well I admit that fooling's a funny kind of game, no rhyme and no reason, but then,
There are things that you can do when you are only a clown, so I'll have that verse over again:
One day as I was a-tumbling I saw them planting trees all day
And taking apart that monster machine and dancing all the days away. *Chorus*

When I woke up this morning it was you I was dreaming about,
But the white rabbits bowed and put on their hats and told me it's time to go out.
Well I've only made a start on the fooling; you'll have to put me through the fooling school.
Although twelve o'clock has passed and gone, I'm still an April fool. *Chorus*

Green Jack

Wind to north east, snow on the crest,
Winter takes a long time to be gone.
Lambs in the fold, safe from the cold,
April past and May coming on;
But pray lend an ear this music to hear,
Cold winds be gone, give Jack but a chance.
Hey come along, hey come along,
Come along and join in the dance.

O have you seen Jack in the Green
Footing it so lightly on his toes,
Buds on the trees, blossom and leaves
Springing out wherever he goes?
For he who was slain
With the harvested grain
Is born anew and bids summer advance.
Hey come along, hey come along,
Come along and join in the dance.

Birdsong at dawn, up with the morn,
Throwing off the years by two and three,
Old Mrs Jones stretches her bones
And puts the whistling kettle on for tea.
Then she sweeps up the dirt and she gathers her skirt
And away with Green Jack she does prance.
Hey come along, hey come along,
Come along and join in the dance.

Morris men all, squire and the fool
Cut a merry caper on the green.
Come maids and young men, let the dancing begin
For the living earth our fair queen.
Then footing it still make a ring round the hill
And light up the sky with your chants.
Hey come along, hey come along,
Come along and join in the dance.

O have you seen Jack in the Green
Footing it so lightly on his toes,
Buds on the trees, blossom and leaves
Springing out wherever he goes?
For he who was slain,
Like the harvested grain
Is born anew and bids summer advance.
Hey come along, hey come along,
Come along and join in the dance.

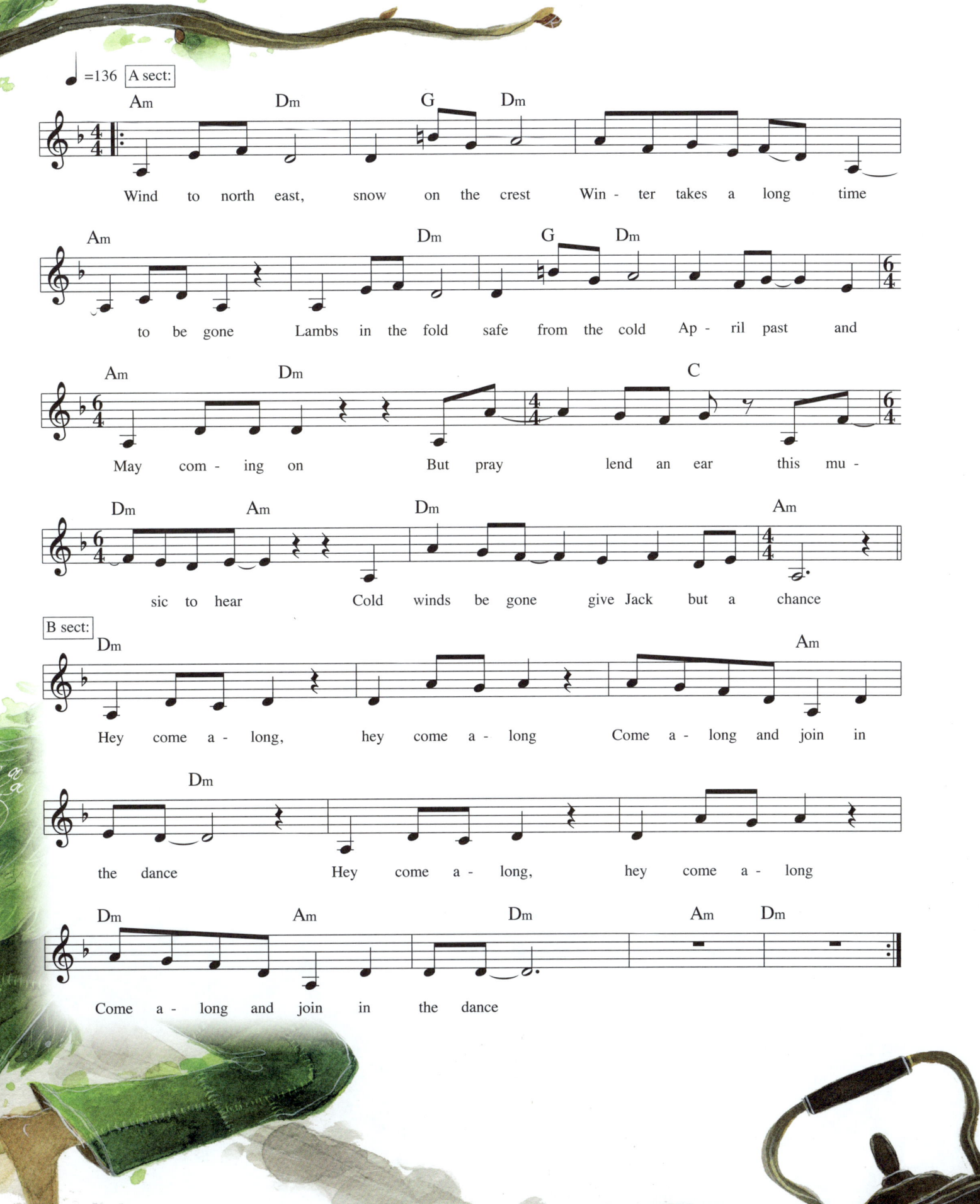

Herb Song

Summertime, stretch out in the sun,
Spread out your arms, feel the earth is breathing.
Light in the air pours copper on your hair,
Gold on your arm and your shoulder gleaming.

Parsley, tarragon, fennel and savory,
Lavender baskets for the making,
Rosemary, marjoram, dill and sweet cicely,
Lemon balm when your heart is aching.

Down in the stream the water is cool,
Rats go scudding in the lush green rushes.
Shrimps and shiny black water bugs tickle you.
Brace your legs where the current is strong. *Chorus*

Take my hand and we'll walk out in the sun.
Spread out your soul and you'll feel it floating.
Harvest the sky, scents and colours on the wind.
Store the seeds carefully for next year's sowing. *Chorus*

June Morning

The juggernauts are pounding the Old Port road with scrap from the foundry yard
And the river slips under the car park bridge with little white flowers in its beard
And the morning's like a new born baby with a golden dawn around its head
And the moment spins between my fingers, can't you feel
The gentle pull on the thread,
All the way to where you are?
All the way to where you are.

The sun is warm on top of the old stone wall, there are roses growing round my feet.
A gentleman is walking his Afghan hound on the other side of the street
And there's somebody standing beside me, whose face I seem to recognise.
It's amazing the way that you keep looking out at me
Through so many strangers' eyes,
While summer's greening on the trees,
While summer's greening on the trees.

The swifts are busy circling on streamlined wings and the buses rumble down the hill.
There's a lady leaning over her garden gate waiting for the day to stand still,
So she can catch up on yesterday's gossip before it slips into the cracks of time,
But if she only knew I am sitting on the spot
That marks today's dateline
And time is tangled in my hair,
And time is tangled in my hair.

The river's slipping under the Old Port bridge but the time it hasn't slipped away.
It's right in the heart of this red rose bud if I choose to see it that way.
Though the foundry's still rattling and churning and the lady's leaning over her gate
Still the moment spins between my fingers, can't you feel
The gentle pull on the thread,
All the way to where you are?
All the way to where you are.

The Smell of New Hay

When the sun is too scarce and the wind from north west
And rough weathers, storm weathers batter July,
The grasses grow tall and heavy with rain
And we long for the light and the smell of new hay.
For sweetness mown down, lying close to the ground,
Yes, we long for the smell of new hay,
Hay, hay, smell of new hay,
We long for the smell of new hay.

Now midsummer's passed by, all wet chill and cold
And the meadows are full with a tangle of green.
Our limbs have grown idle, we've forgotten the skills,
To cut, toss and turn and to bring the hay in,
With scythe and with rake, with pitch fork and wain,
To gather the sweet harvest in,
Harvest in, sweet harvest in.
To gather the sweet harvest in.

We are troubled and torn, cannot wake, cannot sleep.
The ripeness is stretching the rims of the day.
But it's never too late to be learning anew
To go pacing and swinging out into the hay.
We are labourers all and this is our joy,
To go swinging out into the hay,
Hay, hay, into the hay
To go swinging out into the hay.

Here's the song of the scythe in the heat of the day,
For time's on the turn and tomorrow's unknown;
At the dance of the blade the grasses lie down
And gently surrender their life to the ground,
Oh softly the grass lies whispering down
And surrenders its life to the ground,
Ground, ground, life to the ground,
And surrenders its life to the ground.

The Corn King

I am the corn king, rich in seed,
Diving into the earth when the year is young.
In her secret dark I seethe and grow,
'Til the furrows burn green with my life begun.

I am king of the corn, I am the corn king,
I am the corn king, I am.

Tossed by the wind and fed by the rain
I ripen and swell when the summer is high;
Then acres wide I stand and turn
Tall and gold beneath the sky.   *Chorus*

Once cockles and cornflowers bloomed among
The crinkled poppies in their blood red tide,
But the grain still fattens and my stems grow long
As I dream of the cutting at harvest tide.   *Chorus*

Then you come with your blades, you come with your wheels,
Shearing me through just under the knee;
Then you thresh and batter me 'til I'm clean
So the miller may grind the flour from me.   *Chorus*

The baker he kneads me up and then down
And leaves me to prove in the good brown bowl;
Then into the oven until I am done.
I am bread in your basket and food for your soul.   *Chorus*

My ears are as many as stars in the sky.
I dance in the fields as the wind blows by.
The stars and the earth cast glyphs and runes
In my ripening corn and you wonder why.   *Chorus*

This was written in response to a communication with a wheat field by Silbury Hill which contained a Mayan design crop circle. I went there in the rain in July 2009 with friends and was surprised that it was the meeting with the wheat which affected me most deeply. It needed to be honoured.

Harvest Festival

There's a shift in the weather, there are holes in my memory,
There are gaps in the branches for the ripe fruit to fall through,
And somewhere inside me the good soil is waiting,
For the thoughts we have dared, love,
For the dreams we have shared, love,
For the love we have seeded to take root and grow,
For the love we have seeded to take root and grow.

I am watching the days fall, slipping down through my fingers.
Let them spin, let them tumble to the darkness underneath;
And the woman inside me sees the leaves on the water,
Sees the ripples of choices, the gains and the losses,
But she feels no confusion, there is harvest in her eyes,
She feels no confusion, there is harvest in her eyes.

Farewell to the budding, farewell to the flowering.
The great tide receding leaves the shore clean and empty,
And the woman goes barefoot, her heart full with ripeness,
And she scatters it broadcast, there is no more escaping.
For the seed there is nowhere, nowhere to go but down,
For the seed there is nowhere, nowhere to go but down.

There's a shift in the wea-ther, there are holes in my mem-or-y There are
gaps in the branch-es for the ripe fruit to fall through And
some where in-side me the good soil is wait-ing For the thoughts we have
dared, love For the dreams we have shared, love For the love we have
seed-ed to take root and grow For the love we have
seed-ed to take root and
grow I am...

Shooting Stars

The corn is all in and the fields they are bare;
There are berries on the bramblethorn,
And the crossback spinners are spinning away
To be ready for the dew in the morn,
And the greedy great combine's shut up in the barn,
And the farmer runs his fingers through the mounds of new corn,
And the sun is rolling down along the roofs of the town,
And I'm waiting for the shooting stars. *Repeat*

The last of the stubble will soon be turned in;
To the plough the good soil now must yield,
And the hare streaks away with the late blackbird's song,
Like a shadow on the darkening field,
And the lights are coming on in the windows of the town,
And the smell of the earth is like the snatches of a song
That my heart went on singing long after you'd gone,
But now I'm waiting for the shooting stars. *Repeat*

Through a gap in the blackthorn I slip through the hedge
And away from all the passing cars.
On the edge of the stubble the moon has come up,
Pale boat above the shadowy trees,
And suddenly the stars come shooting, blazing down,
All over the bare fields and the houses in the town,
And the air is all aglow with shimmering corn,
And there's a Lady sowing stars for grain. *Repeat*

There's a rattling of leaves at the side of the road,
And I'm standing on the verge of a dream.
Was it mist in the trees or the line of a cloud?
She was standing on the curving moon;
But the corn that she sowed it was real golden grain,
And somewhere a nightingale is starting to sing,
And I know that I shall see you again in the spring.
I can read it in the shooting stars. *Repeat*

The corn is all in and the fields they are bare There are
berries on the bramble thorn And the cross-back spinners are
spinning away To be ready for the dew in the morn And the
greedy great combine's shut up in the barn And the
farmer runs his fingers through the mounds of new corn And the
sun is running down along the roofs of the town And I'm
waiting for the shooting stars And I'm waiting for the shooting

Violin: Voice:

stars

(The...)

Autumn into Winter

As I went out one rainy morning
All in the cloud and the winter wind
The sky was grey and the leaves were falling
Upon the dark and the muddy ground.
'Twas there I spied a fair young damsel
Her face it shone like some candle flame,
'Oh come you here my charming creature
And let me shield you from the rain.'

'Kind Sir', she said, 'of your good favour,
Protect me now from the wind so wild,
For I am weary of the weather,
And besides I am with child.
Oh can you tell of any shelter,
Where I may sit down before the fire
And rest myself and my tender burden
All from the road and from the mire.'

'Pray take my coat, my dearest lady.
With right good will do I give it you.'
And so I put my arms about her
As along the road we both did go.
I led her to my humble cottage,
Bade her sit down herself to warm.
The lamp I kindled from the fire,
To keep the damsel from all harm.

So while the wind blew all its fury
And the rain and gale did tear up the night,
Protected there from any tempest
We sat before the fire bright.
My heart to her I then did offer,
While outside the window sang the storm.
She accepted me and I vowed to love her
And I'll bless the day when that babe is born.

So come all you people that go a-walking
Along the road in the winter wind,
If you should chance to meet a stranger
In bitter need then be not unkind.
For treasure lies where 'tis least expected,
Though days be hard and the road be long,
And love is born in the darkest moment
When life is sheerest and hope forlorn.

For treasure lies where 'tis least expected
Catch the first phrase as you travel on,
For music's born out of storm and struggle
And here's the starting of my song.

As I went out one rainy morning All in the cloud and the winter wind The sky was grey and the leaves were falling Upon the dark and the muddy ground 'Twas there I spied a fair young damsel Her face it shone like some candle flame 'Oh come you here my charming creature And let me shield you from the rain' Kind...

Winter Solstice

It's four o'clock and it's almost dark
The darkness falls so soon today
The swings are empty in the park
Cold winter's on its way

But it's time to pass around the bowl
And it's lighting up time in my soul
For the winter solstice

The leaves are trodden on the ground
So many hopes have fluttered down
Sometimes I don't know where I'm bound
And the path is hard to see

But if trees could talk then they would tell
How the leaves were blazing as they fell
With hidden fire

The doors are shut and the curtains drawn
Cold winter locked out in the street
The hours seem endless to the dawn
And the stars so far away

But every star is listening
To hear what music we shall bring
To the winter solstice

The seed lies buried in the ground
The longest night will be soon be done
As the year begins another round
The seed begins to grow

Then the dawn will chase the dark away
And the bells ring out the livelong day
On Christmas morning

It's four o'clock and it's almost dark
The darkness falls so soon today
The swings are empty in the park
Cold winter's on its way

But it's time to pass around the bowl
And it's lighting up time in my soul
For the winter solstice

♩=139
A sect:
A D E A
It's four o' clock and it's al - most dark The
A D A E A D
dark - ness falls so soon to - day The swings are emp - ty
B sect:
E A D E A E
in the park Cold wint - er's on its way But it's time to pass a - round
D A E D E
the bowl And it's light - ing up time in my soul
E D E A
For the win - ter sol - stice (The)

Bells at Midnight

Oh tell how the trees are grim and bare
And sharp the frost on dale and mountain,
While sheep turn their backs against the wind,
That shakes the brown and scanty grazing.
And men pull their hats about their ears
And hard at their heels stalk winter fears:
'Oh when shall we ever see the sun,
And when will these hard times be done?'
But care with the bells at midnight flees away
And joy comes in on Christmas morning.

And in her icy furrow sits the hare,
The stormy blast about her beating.
But she fears not the frozen fields so bare
For courage will find her winter feeding.
So why should we fear the winter's cold
When under the furrow sleeps the gold?
The Earth bears the seed of future sun
And out of the dark new life will come,
When care with the bells at midnight flees away
And joy comes in on Christmas morning.

So sweep the hearth clean and lay the fire
And welcome each friend and stranger passing,
And spread a fine cloth upon the board
With nuts and fruit for Christmas feasting.
And forget not the steaming cup to share
And songs to delight the heart and ear.
Every soul a candle now shall light
To welcome the child that's born tonight
For care with the bells at midnight flees away
And joy comes in on Christmas morning.

Oh tell how the trees are grim and bare And sharp the frost on dale and mountain While sheep turn their backs against the wind That shakes the brown and scanty grazing And men pull their hats about their ears And hard at their heels stalk winter fears: 'Oh when shall we ever see the sun, And when shall these hard times be done?' But care with the bells at midnight flees away And joy comes in on Christmas morning and in her...

Jehanne Mehta and husband Rob shaped a musical genre that captured the spirit of the time. They were able to embed and evoke within the music a conscience for action towards the living earth, bringing together not only the joy and celebration of the natural world but also the insights and responsibility to co-shape its future. Their music is born out of locality, but strikes a worldwide chord of appreciation and insight.

Aonghus Gordon OBE, Ruskin Mill Trust

Activism

People of the Earth

We are the people of the Earth.

Our kinfolks are the dogwood and the maple;
The hickory and the pine our brothers too,
And our footfalls leave no traces across the secret places
And we know where the deer and beaver go.

We climb the mountain trails in the morning
To greet the sun arising in the east;
And to hear the little birds singing praises without words
For the life that springs in every feathered breast.

And we watch the dog star rising in the evening,
And we understand the voices of the trees,
And the song the river sings and the swish of eagles' wings.
There is language to be heard in every breeze.

But now you come to ravage and to plunder
And to rape the darkness of your mother's womb.
You destroy our holy mountains with no reckoning nor accounting
How you turn her living body to the tomb.

And you use her bones for fuel to make power,
That can burn and poison every living thing,
Bringing sickness, death and sorrow and more to come tomorrow.
Could be soon there will be nothing left to sing.

And you use her secret structures for your profit;
Claim ownership of every living thing.
Now the precious soil is dying and fewer birds are flying.
Could be soon there will be nothing left to sing.

[continued overleaf]

♩=74 **A sect: (Verse 1, 2, 3, 8, 9)**

| Am | Dm | Am | Dm | Em |

We are the peo-ple of the Earth   Our kin-folks are the dog-wood and the

| Am | | G | C | Em |

ma-ple   The hickory and the pine our broth-ers too   And our

| Am | Em | Dm | Em |

foot-falls leave no tra-ces   a-cross the sec-ret pla-ces And we

| Am | Em | Am | Em |

know where the deer and beav-er go

B sect: (Verse 4, 5, 6, 7)

| Am | Em | Am | Em |

(But) now you come to rav-age and to plun-der   And to

| Am | Dm | Em |

rape the dark-ness of your moth-er's womb   You des-

| Am | Dm | Am | Em |

troy our ho-ly moun-tains, with no reck'ning or ac-count-ing How you

| Am | Em | Am | Em |

turn her liv-ing bo-dy to the tomb

Ending (8):

| Am | Em | Am | Dm | Am Dm Am |

We are the peo-ple of the Earth..................

Now you threaten all the children of the future,
And the creatures of the earth and of the air,
With electric radiation and rays of strong pulsation
And there will be no place of safety anywhere.

O put your feet down gentle on the mountain,
O put your feet down gentle on the Earth;
For you know she is your mother and there'll never be another
To sustain you every moment from your birth.

We are the keepers of the Earth.
We guard her hidden gateways to the dawn.
In the silence of her shadows, on her bluffs and in her hollows,
Until the day of brotherhood shall come.

We are the people of the Earth.

51

Blue Whale

In the lap of the ocean the great whale was born,
Off the Congo River coast in the heart of a storm,
In the tumult of waves and the scream of the gale;
A hard start but fitting for a two-ton young whale.

Hear me now, oh hear my call,
Mile after mile through the echoing swell.
Won't you hear my call, don't you hear me now?
I'll tell of the passing of the mighty blue whale.

Farewell to the warm seas off Africa's shore,
To the currents and canyons I may never hear more,
Where the humpback whales sing and the dolphins they play.
I'm bound for South Georgia to feed or to die. *Chorus*

Farewell to the sun on the rippling wave,
Where in peace a young whale he may roll, dive and play,
To Atlantean mountains unfathomed and steep,
Where our call echoes lonely across the salt deep. *Chorus*

If men they are lonely on the far open sea,
How lonesome is the whale that is bound for to die?
Across wild wastes of ocean I may seek for a mate,
But what joy in the wedding if death be our fate? *Chorus*

O South Georgia lies over east from the horn,
Bleak, ice bound and barren in the dark winter storm,
But in summer the whales break their fast on the krill,
And the factory ships scream as they slice up their kill. *Chorus*

There are none there to weep, there are none there to cry,
There are times when it takes a full hour to die.
There's no way to escape the cruel watery doom,
Torn apart by a six-foot exploding harpoon. *Chorus*

A sect: *a capella*

In the lap of the ocean the great whale was born Off the Congo River coast in the heart of a storm In the tumult of waves and the scream of the gale A hard start but fitting for a two ton young whale

B sect:

Hear me now, oh hear my call Mile after mile through the echoing swell Won't you hear my call, don't you hear me now? I'll tell of the passing of the mighty blue whale (Fare-

This Power

Tell me where is this power bred?
Or in the heart or in the head?
How begot, how nourishèd?
It is engendered in the skull
In that dark place where death do dwell.
In empty sockets, staring eyes
In milk-white bone the serpent lies
'Tis there that power's bred.

Tell me how does this power feed?
It feeds on money, feeds on greed.
It kills the life within the seed.
It feeds on weakness, feeds on fear.
It whispers comforts in your ear:
We need the jobs, we need to feel
Protected in our old life-style;
There's no end to our needs.

Tell me where does this power go?
Tell me how to mark its flow
In air and in the earth below.
It goes to make the deadly bombs.
It gets into your very bones.
It poisons land and poisons sea
From now until eternity.
And none can flee the fire.

Tell me how is this power won?
It's won through the barrel of a gun
And the intercontinental run.
It's won with the silos underground
And the cruise missiles that move around.
With apathy and lack of trust
As we stand before the final test,
We unleash the dogs of war.

Now what is the message in the wind?
Can power be gentle, power be kind
Or must it warp and twist the mind?
Imagination roaming free
Gives eyes our limits for to see.
The only hope for a better start
Is power rising from the heart.
O, can we turn the tide?

♩=158

Tell me where is this pow-er bred? Or in the heart or in the head? How be-got, how nour-ish-èd? It is en-gen-dered in the skull In that dark place where death do dwell In emp-ty sock-ets, star-ing eyes In milk-white bone the ser-pent lies 'Tis there that pow-er's bred

Lament for the Trees

The summer is gone and it's harvesting time
And fat bales of wheat straw all stand in a line.
The trailers are rumbling home with the grain
And the roaring of dryers is heard in the barn.
But I'll sing a lament for the trees.
Red clover and yarrow still bloom on the verge
And ripe fruits and berries are thick in the hedge.
Apples and plum clusters hang on the bough.
Take the harvester into the ripe barley now.
There's no time to think about trees.

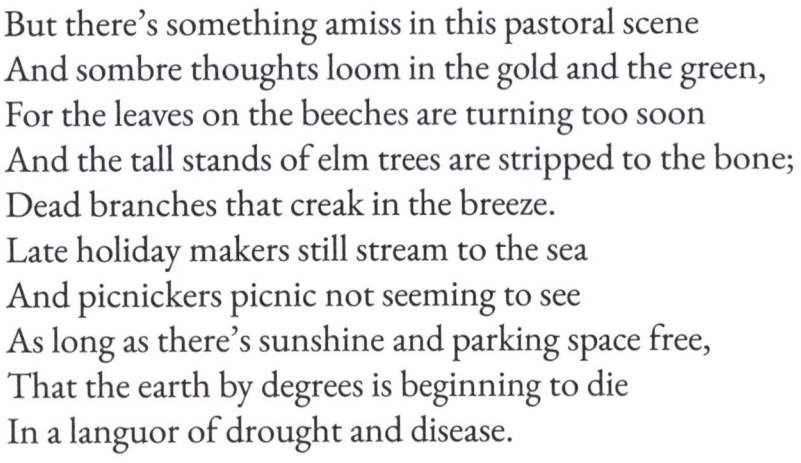

But there's something amiss in this pastoral scene
And sombre thoughts loom in the gold and the green,
For the leaves on the beeches are turning too soon
And the tall stands of elm trees are stripped to the bone;
Dead branches that creak in the breeze.
Late holiday makers still stream to the sea
And picnickers picnic not seeming to see
As long as there's sunshine and parking space free,
That the earth by degrees is beginning to die
In a languor of drought and disease.

We've had enough rain this year, harvest is good.
If fine weather lasts we'll be out of the woods
And we've dammed up the streams, there'll be nothing to fear
If we should have drought like the one t'other year.
If there's time we'll cut down the dead trees.
If there's talk of disease we have liquids and sprays.
For most forms of blight there are methods and ways
Of protecting the crops and increasing the yield.
We've a living to make from meadow and field;
There's not much we can do about trees.

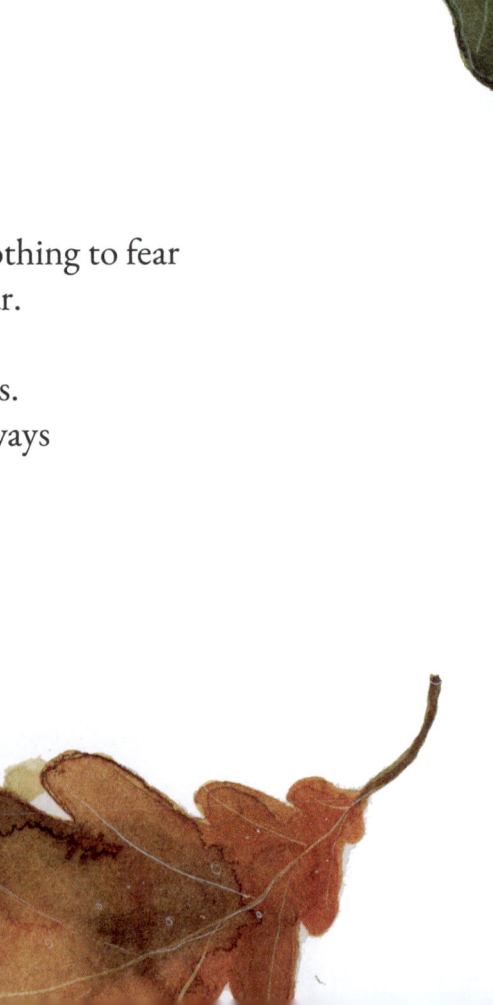

[continued overleaf]

♩=146 [A sect:]

The summer is gone and it's har-vest-ing time And
fat bales of wheat straw all stand in a line The
trail-ers are rum-bling home with the grain And the roar-ing of
dry-ers is heard in the barn But I'll sing a lam-ent

[B sect:]

for the trees Red clo-ver and yar-row still
bloom on the verge And ripe fruits and ber-ries are thick in the hedge
Ap-ples and plum clus-ters hang on the bough Take the
har-vest-er in-to the ripe bar-ley now There's no time to
think a-bout trees But there's

But drought in the heart and disease in the soul,
They shrivel the roots and eat into the bole
And blindness of heart in the suffering soil
Brings rot and decay and dry brown leaves that curl
In a dying that nobody sees.
We are dust of Earth's dust and bone of her bone;
She gives us our nourishment, shelter and home.
In enriching ourselves we have ravaged the Earth;
We should wonder if she can go on giving birth.
O lament the slow death of the trees.

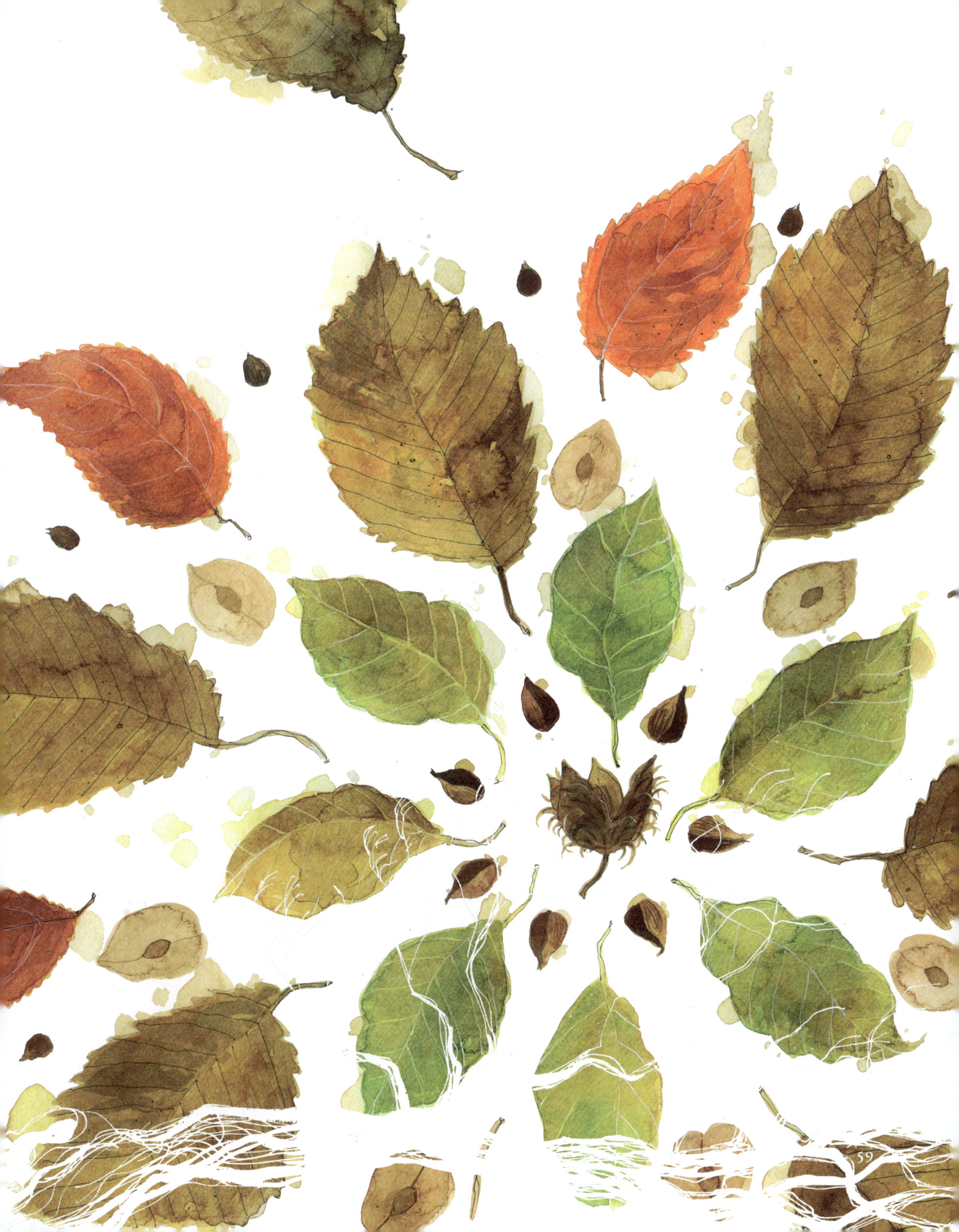

Bobbin of Yarn

Oh the battle was o'er and the people were coming
To succour the wounded and bury the dead,
But the prisoner was sent to a far distant country,
With a chain round his ankle and a band round his head;
And close by the shore his love sat waiting
A-hoping her Johnny had come to no harm,
And as she sat there fine wool she was winding,
A-spinning so finely a bobbin of yarn.

'Twas there she espied his companions returning,
'Your Johnny's not here, though we know he's not dead,
But we fear he's been sent to a far distant country
With a chain round his ankle and a band round his head.'
'How can I sit here and wait, my Johnny,
Not knowing if ever I'll see you return?'
So she's gone aboard ship to sail over the ocean,
With a knife in her belt and a bobbin of yarn.

Oh strong winds they did blow and the seas they were rolling
All over the decks as they ploughed through the storm,
But love is a light that will guide a ship well
And she sailed into port at the breaking of dawn.
'Oh whether he's near or far my Johnny
Shall languish no longer in fear or alarm.'
And Sally's away in search of her lover
With a knife in her belt and a bobbin of yarn.

Oh the gates they were strong and the wires they were sharp.
There were weapons above and under the ground;
And over them all many prisoners stood guarding
The fences of fear that were stretched all around.
And Johnny's cried out as he stood on watch
And young Johnny's cried out as he lay on his bed,
'How can I recall what it was I was seeking,
With a chain round my ankle and a band round my head?'

[continued overleaf]

♪=180 **A sect:**

Oh the bat-tle was o'er and the peo-ple were com-ing To
Suc-cour the wound-ed and bur-y the dead But the pris-on-er was sent to a
far dis-tant coun-try With a chain round his an-kle and a

B sect:

band round his head And close by the shore his love sat wait-ing A-
hop-ing her John-ny had come to no harm And as she sat there fine
wool she was wind-ing A- spin-ning so fine-ly a

Violin: Voice:

bob-bin of yarn   (It was)

Oh when she came nigh where her Johnny was standing,
He was sick to the heart and troubled in mind
For thinking some ill might befall his dear Sally,
But she gave him a sign with a wave of her hand.
In the dead of the night, when the foe lay a-sleeping,
Never thinking their fortress could e'er be torn down,
With her little penknife she cut through the wires
And she started unwinding her bobbin of yarn.

And it's over and under betwixt and between
How she circled that fortress around and around,
'Til nought could be seen but a shine and a shimmer
Of thread upon thread drifting over the ground.
'Come away with me now for your chains are all broken
And the band round your forehead is shattered and gone,
And the fences of fear are all blowing away
And it's all by the work of my bobbin of yarn.

Come away with me now for your chains are all broken
And the band round your forehead is shattered and gone,
And the fences of fear are all blowing away
And it's all by the work of my bobbin of yarn,
And it's all by the work of my bobbin of yarn.'

The bobbin of yarn is an image of female sexuality in folk tradition, but I have used it in the sense of a magical creative force here. This song was inspired by Greenham Common Women's Peace Camp in the early 1980s.

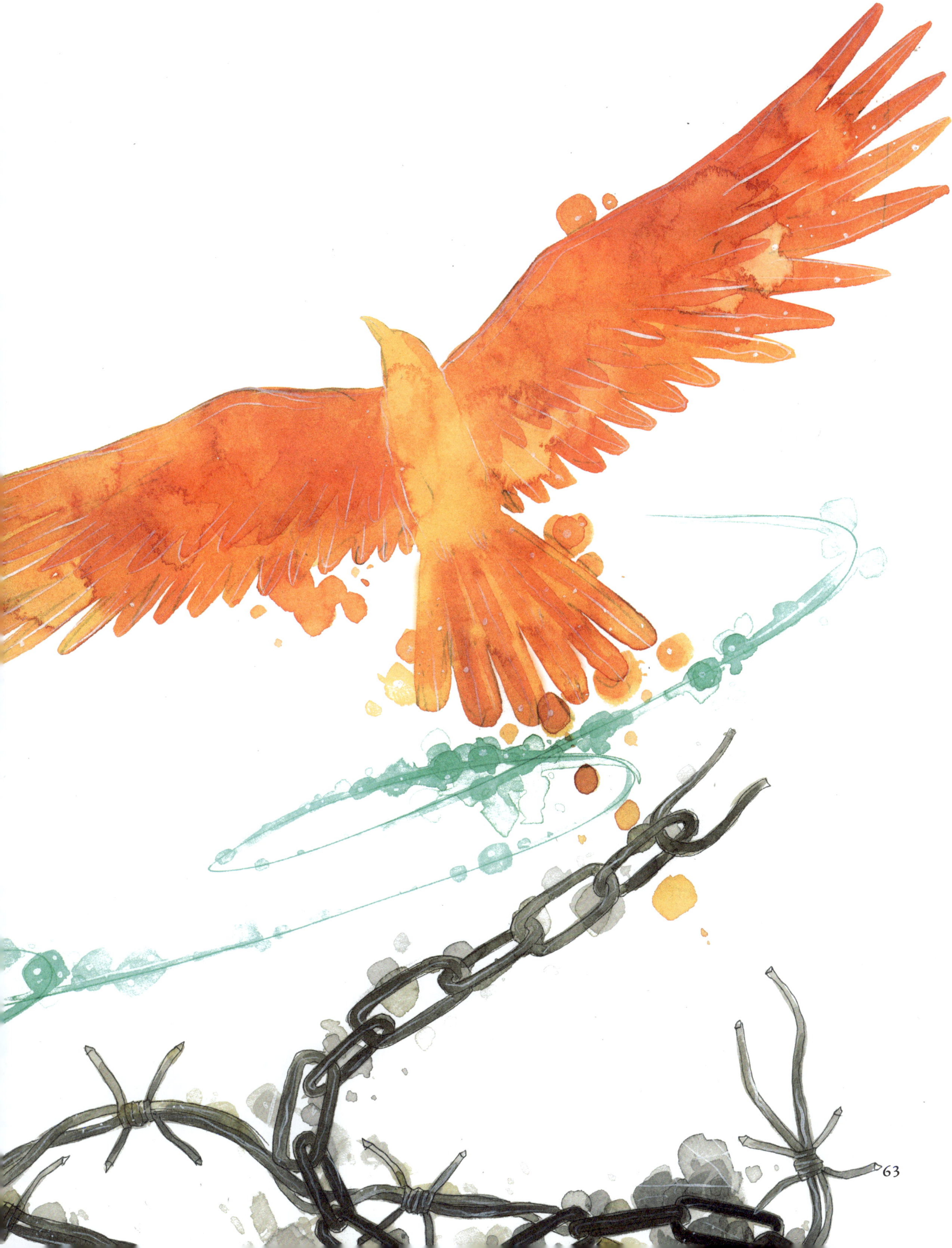

Make my Peace

When first we fell in love so many thousand years ago
I worshipped the very ground on which you stood,
And to look into your face left an aching in my heart
And your touch spoke in the rhythms of my blood;
But time and ambition can blind a lover's eye
And somehow I lost sight of you as the years went rolling by
But now I want to make my peace with you, Lady,
Now I want to make my peace with you.

The tortoiseshells are basking on the old lock walls
And the ash keys hang in clusters by the stream,
Where on every sandy bar there's a bottle or a can
And the banks are tangled up with polythene,
And the foundry slag's invaded where the orchard used to stand
And there's litter on the footpath in the grass on either hand
And it's high time to make my peace again with you, Lady,
Oh yes it's time to make my peace with you.

You used to provide with no effort on my part
And I was strong and flourished in your arms,
And I'd bring you little presents to show you that I cared
And you'd flash a sudden smile of piercing charm;
But I needed independence so I shut myself away,
Didn't notice the distance growing larger every day,
But now I want to make my peace again with you, Lady,
Now I want to make my peace with you.

There are tidy little houses all across the countryside
Where once the lark rose, singing, to the sky.
There are neat little containers rumbling down the railway line
Carrying radioactive waste down to the sea.
There are miles of empty desert where the forests used to roll.
I made use of your body but forgot you had a soul,
So now I want to make my peace again with you, Lady,
Now I want to make my peace with you.

[continued overleaf]

When first we fell in love so many thousand years ago I worshipped the very ground on which you stood And to look into your face left an aching in my heart And your touch spoke in the rhythms of my blood But time and ambition can blind a lover's eye And somehow I lost sight of you as the years went rolling by But now I want to make my peace again with you, Lady Now I want to make my peace with you

The...

When first we fell in love so many thousand years ago,
I worshipped the very ground on which you stood,
And to look into your face left an aching in my heart
And your touch spoke in the rhythms of my blood.
Tonight I saw a rainbow stretching right across the sky
Maybe it's not to late to have another try
So now I want to make my peace again with you, Lady,
Now I want to make my peace with you.

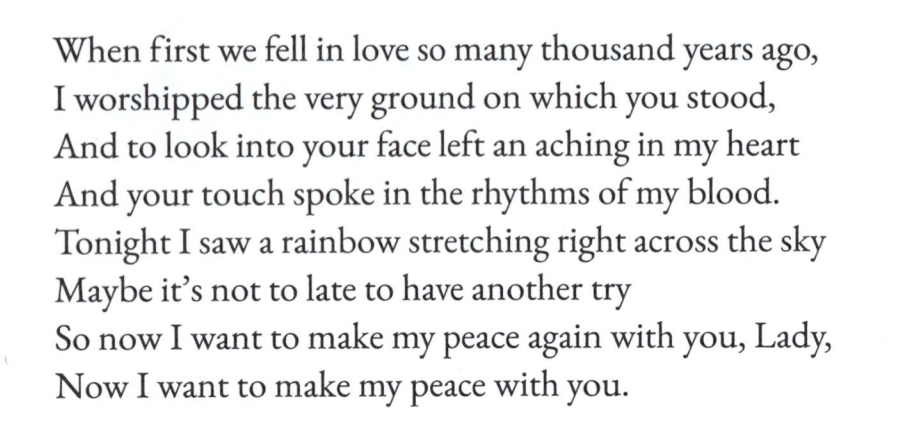

This song was sung at the opening of Ruskin Mill College.

67

Stop the World

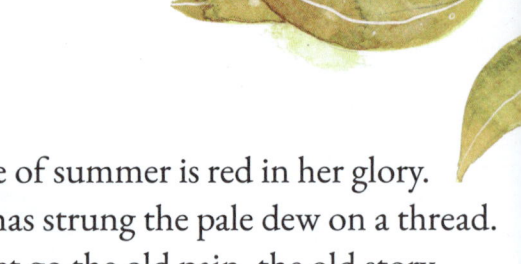

Let the wind go wherever it wanders.
Strip your soul back bare to the bone.
Give to the wind all your plans and agendas.
Stop the world,
Stop the world,
Stop the world, I want to get on,
Stop the world, I want to get on.

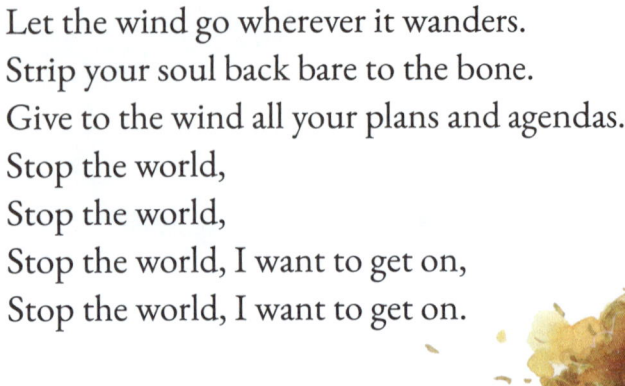

The ash falls in sprays,
The oak tree in singles.
Strip your soul back bare to the bone.
The sycamore flames
And burns up like a candle.
Stop the world,
Stop the world,
Stop the world, I want to get on,
Stop the world, I want to get on.

All that is real is your heart and its changes,
On the edge of the hill to the beat of the gale,
While the old worm tries to hold on to his prizes,
Need in his eyes and a sting in his tail,
With need in his eyes and a sting in his tail.

Let the wind go wherever it wanders.
Strip your soul back bare to the bone.
Give to the wind all your plans and agendas.
Stop the world,
Stop the world,
Stop the world, I want to get on,
Stop the world, I want to get on.

The last rose of summer is red in her glory.
The spider has strung the pale dew on a thread.
O will you let go the old pain, the old story
And start every day with a new one instead?
And start every day with a new one instead.

All that is real is your heart and its changes.
You don't need a chisel to open a rose.
These songs are all free
You can take them or leave them.
The words that you hear
Are the words that you choose.
The words that you hear
Are the words that you choose.

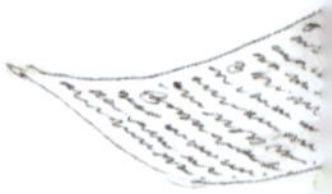

Let the wind go wherever it wanders.
Strip your soul back bare to the bone.
Give to the wind all your plans and agendas.
Stop the world,
Stop the world,
Stop the world, I want to get on,
Stop the world, I want to get on.

♩=120 | A sect:

D / **G** / **D** / **G**
Let the wind go wher-ev-er it wand-ers   Strip your soul back

G **A** / **D** **G** **D**
bare to the bone   Give to the wind all your plans and ag-end-as

G A **G** **D/F#** **Em** **D/F#** **G** **A**
Stop the world   Stop the world   Stop the world, I want to get on Stop the

G **A** **D A G A** | B sect: ♩=90 *Rubato* **GMaj7** **D**
world, I want to get on   (The...) All that is real is your

♩=130 *A Tempo*

G **A** **G** **D**
heart and its chang-es   On the edge of the hill to the

D **A** **F#** **G A Bm**
beat of the gale   While the old worm tries to hold on to his priz-es

G─3─ **D** **A**
Need in his eyes and a sting in his tail   With

G─3─ **D** **A** **D A G A**
need in his eyes and a sting in his tail

69

Emblem

Wear your heart like an emblem, like a banner, like a flower,
Bright on a field of argent, bright on a field of gold.
Carry it before you, like a herald, like a herald,
Like a horn that you are winding as the front line comes on.

Wear your heart like a sun, whose face is unhidden,
Whose rays are like hands that bless although they burn,
Like a joy that is open, even when its petals, falling, drifting,
Dye the plains with purple and its robe is torn.

Wear your heart like a coin of bright copper, that will pay
For every passage you may venture to place your foot upon.
Wear it like a vessel, like a cup that you are sharing,
Though not knowing if your journeying will ever reach a home.

And all the while the river turns,
From the centre to the shore and back
And all the while your beating heart
Is the keeper of the keys.

And all the while the river turns
From the centre to the shore and back
And all the while your beating heart
Is the keeper of the keys.

Wear your heart like a beacon that you raise to rouse the sleepers,
The dreamers in their labyrinths of nerve and blood and bone.
Wear it like a song you will never finish singing.
You know all the earth is listening for your heart's song,
You know all the earth is listening for your heart's song.

♩=118 A sect (Verse 1, 2 3, 6):

Gm — Wear your heart like an em-blem like a ban-ner, Gm like a flower

Gm — Bright on a field of ar-gent Gm Bright on a field of go-ld B♭ F

B♭ — Car-ry it be-fore you, like a F her-ald, like a B♭ her-ald Like a horn

E♭ — that you are win-ding Gm as the front line F comes on

B sect (Verse 4, 5): ♩=135 D — And all the while the ri-ver turns Gm From the

D cen-tre to the E♭Maj7 shore and back E♭ And all the while your D beat-ing heart

D is the E♭Maj7 keep-er of the keys D

Lord in the Green

I am beech, ash and oak.
I am the giants with no name.
You fell me with fire and the saw.
I am healer to the air,
Twin brother to the rain.
Call me Lord in the Green,
Call me Lord in the Green.

Cutting off at ground level,
Cutting off at the root,
Shut out the vertical dimension:
You lose sight of the wood,
You lose sight of the wood.
Smooth over the surface,
But there's no depth to the soil,
Cut out the vertical dimension:
Close the door into your soul,
Close the door into your soul.

Strip the leaves from the branches,
Burn the branches to ashes,
Pluck out your own feathers,
Pluck off your own wings.
Unfasten the weather,
Unfasten the wind,
Inherit the hurricane
When you cut me down.

I tree, sheltering, Lord in the Green,
I tree, living wood, Lord in the Green.

I am king in my country,
Taking care of the ground.
When I am gone it will be hard, so hard,
To put any new roots down,
To put any new roots down.

I hold the dyke against the desert,
I catch the stars in my limbs.
There are creatures that curl
In the crook of my arm,
Where the wild bird stoops and sings,
Where the wild bird sings.

Strip the leaves from the branches,
Burn the branches to ashes,
Pluck out your own feathers,
Pluck off your own wings,
Unfasten the weather,
Unfasten the wind,
Inherit the hurricane
When you cut me down. *Chorus*

In leaf wave and wild wind
I will speak to your soul,
I will remind you of the one great tree
That is the frame of the world,
The living frame of the world.
Planting wherever you wander
At every turn in your path,
Restore the vertical dimension,
Become the roots of the Earth,
The new roots of the Earth.

New leaves on new branches,
Like a phoenix from ashes,
Feel the growth of your feathers,
Feel the spread of your wings.
There's a change in the weather,
There's a shift in the wind,
A new climate is opening,
I am rising again. *Chorus*

Repeat first verse

♩=82 A sect: *a capella*

I am beech, ash and oak I am the gi-ants with no name You

fell me with fi-re and the saw I am

heal-er to the air, twin broth-er to the rain Call me

rit..................... Fine

Lord in the Green, call me Lord in the Green

♩=76 B sect: 3 x

| C | G | F | G |

Cut-ting off at ground lev-el Cut-ting off at the root

| C | G | F | G | Am |

Shut out the ver-ti-cal di-men-sion: You lose sight of the wood

| F | G | C | G |

You lose sight of the wood Smooth ov-er the sur-face

| F | G | C | G |

But there's no depth to the soil Cut out the ver-ti-cal dim-en-sion

| F | G | Am | F | G | C |

Close the door in-to your soul Close the door in-to your soul

[music continued overleaf]

| F | C/E | Dm | Am |

Strip the leaves from the branch - es   Burn the branch - es to ash - es

| B♭ | F | G | C |

Pluck out your own feath - ers   Pluck off your own wings

| F | C/E | Dm | Am |

Un - fast - en the weath - er   Un - fast - en the wind

| B♭ | C | B♭/D | C/E F | Am |

In - her - it the hur - ric - ane   When you cut me down   I tree, shel - ter - ing,

| F | C | F | Am | F | G | Am | **D.S.** al Fine |

Lord in the Green   I tree liv - ing wood,   Lord in the Green

75

Her lyrical roots in the troubadour and folk tradition embrace a penetrating contemporary intensity and sensitivity ... a journey, a threshold and an initiation.

Jay Ramsay, poet

Soul's Journey

Humming Top

My humming top has pictures on it.
They disappear when the top spins round.
Instead I see broad bands of colour.
Each one seems to hum a tune.

Green and red and blue and yellow,
Orange, violet whirling round,
All the colours in the rainbow;
Every colour makes a sound.

First comes red, I hear it shouting…
Red for anger, red for shame,
Red for sunsets, red for roses,
Red shoes to go dancing in. *Chorus*

Next comes blue, I hear it crooning…
Blue for sadness, blue for skies,
Blue for smoke and blue for shadows,
Blue a pair of laughing eyes. *Chorus*

Next comes green. I hear it humming…
Green for envy, green for grass;
Children shouting, children running…
A green balloon goes sailing past. *Chorus*

Come out and play! Hear yellow calling:
Golden sunlight…daffodils,
Long yellow hair for the wind to sport in,
Farmyard ducks with yellow bills. *Chorus*

♩=161 A sect:

My humming top has pictures on it They disappear when the top spins round Instead I see broad bands of colour

B sect:

Each one seems to hum a tune Green and red and blue and yellow Orange, violet whirling round All the colours in the rainbow Every colour makes a sound

Love is a Song

Love is a song of recognition
The roar of a giant passing plane
At times a very wild condition
Serious as a children's game

A modern kind of exhibition
Where you are items A to Z
A super sound recording studio
Recording every word you said

And love is a coded radio message
I send to you via outer space
A coloured void of vast dimension
To be filled only by your face

And love is an operating table
With many an aching nerve laid bare
At times a haunted house of echoes
Where I feel your step upon the stair

A crowded impersonal railway station
Where the word seems always to be farewell
And love is a story without conclusion
A voyage to the bottom of a well

And love is a kind of humming silence
A gentle gift on a violent day
A dance of the heart about the centre
Serious as games that children play

And love is a song of recognition
The roar of a giant passing plane
A subtle kind of transformation
Serious as a children's game

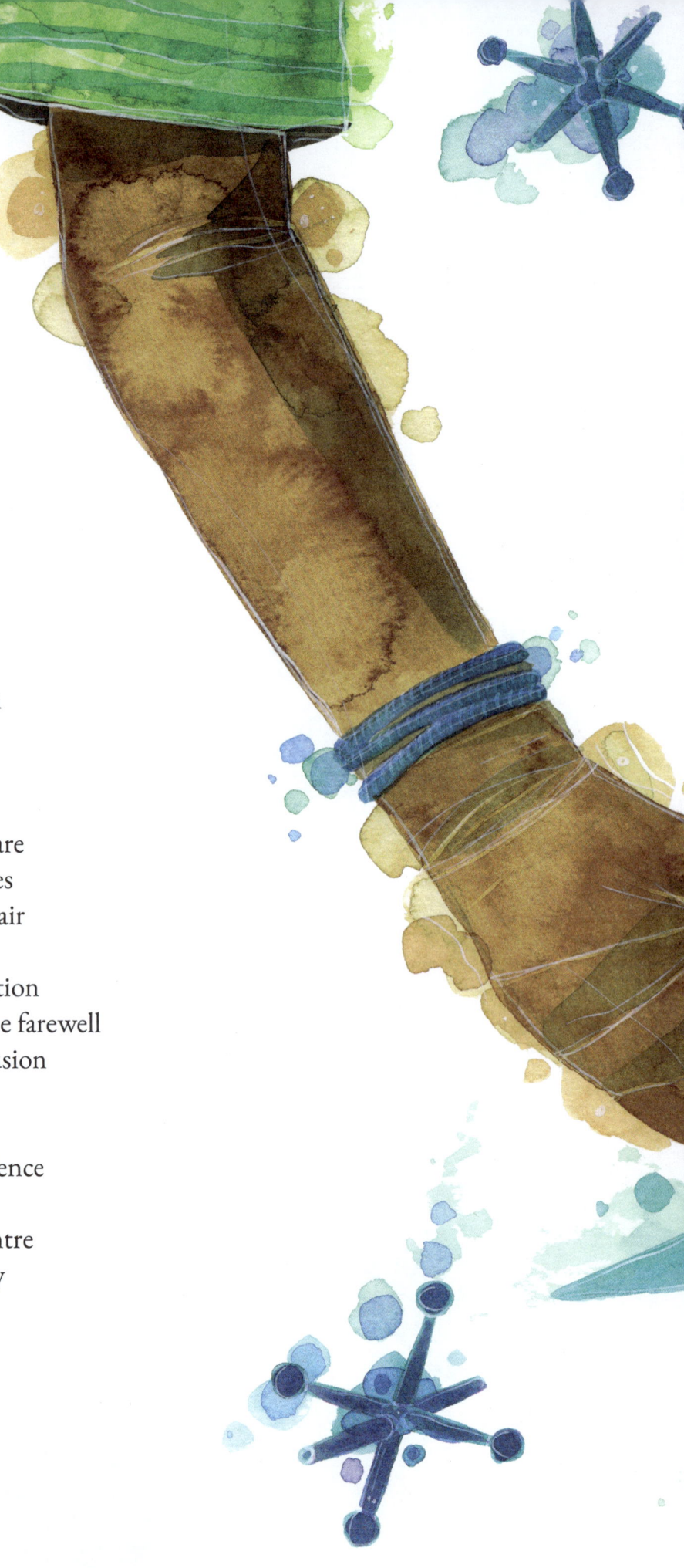

♩=160

Love is a song of re-cog-ni-tion The roar of a gi-ant pass-ing plane At times a ver-y wild con-di-tion Ser-i-ous as a child-ren's game

riten... a tempo

Corridors of Time

There are times in the corridors of time
When the three dimensions seem to shut you in
And you hate the way you've been
And you don't want to go on
And the yellow paint is flaking on the walls,
But there isn't any way out.
You just can't take a day out.
Your yesterdays are stalking in the dark.

There are times when the footsteps on the road
Of people you have passed some time ago
And the ones you're going to meet
All the millions of feet
Will not cease their strident echoes in your ears.
And you'd rather be alone then,
With silence to the bone then,
But that would leave you a prey to all your fears.

So you make time in the spaces of your day
To wrap yourself in layers of soft ash.
An illusion of calm,
Just comfortably warm,
A grey and burnt out refuge in a storm.
But a busker sings a song
And the ashes are all gone
And your heart is plodding naked once again.

But there are times in the corridors of time
When someone singing presses back the pain
And you love the way you've been
And you can't wait to go on
And the walls are thin and easy to pass through.
There are countless ways to go,
So much you want to know
And tomorrow is like sunlight on the sea.

♩=152 A sect:

G — **C**
There are times in the corr-i-doors of time When the

G — **C**
three di-men-sions seem to shut you in And you

Am — **G** — **C**
hate the way you've been And you don't want to go on And the

Dm — **G**
yel-low paint is flak-ing on the walls But there

B sect:

C — **Am** — **C**
is-n't an-y way out You just can't take a day

Am — **G**^{sus4} — **G7**
out Your yes-ter-days are stalk-ing

G7 — **C** — **F** — **C**
in the dark (There are times

Je Me Pardonne

Je me pardonne de m'être trompée de saison,
D'avoir pleuré au lieu de sourire.
De m'être nourrie d'un âpre regime de regret,
D'avoir abandonné l'espoir au souvenir.
Je me pardonne d'avoir étudié avec tant d'acharnement
La poussière de la route déjà parcourue,
Comme si je susciterais des empreintes d'amours fanés
Une douceur que je n'avais jamais connu, que j'ignorais, une douceur que je n'avais jamais connu.

Je me pardonne d'avoir porté si longtemps sur les épaules
Des fardeaux qui ne sont plus les miens,
Pour les craintes que si souvent j'ai lancé devant moi,
Qui assombrissent les roses de mon chemin.
Je me pardonne, de m'être abandonnée moi même sur la route,
Pour partir à la chasse à l'amour,
Pour la surprise de m'être éveillée, un jour triste le coeur vide,
À mes côtés le vertige et la peur, et la peur, à mes côtés le vertige et la peur.

Je me pardonne de m'être trompée de saison,
D'avoir pleuré au lieu de sourire.
De m'être nourrie d'un âpre régime de regret,
D'avoir abandonné l'espoir au souvenir.
Je me pardonne, je m'accepte, je m'enfonce dans cet instant,
Qui me tend ses richesses et son éclat.
Je ne chercherai plus la source dans le monde.
C'est en moi que je puise la joie, que j'avais perdu, c'est en moi que je puise la joie.

Je me pardonne, je me pardonne
Pour la sècheresse que j'ai laissé régner en moi.
Abreuvée par les larmes que je découvre dans mon coeur,
La terre sèche reverdira sur mon chemin, la terre sèche reverdira.

Je me pardonne, je m'accepte, je plonge dans cet instant,
Qui me tend son parfum et son éclat.
Je ne chercherai plus la source dans le monde,
C'est en moi que je puise la joie, que j'avais perdu,
C'est en moi que je puise la joie qui s'était caché, c'est en moi que je puise la joie.

♩=118 **A sect:**

Rubato

Je me Par - don - ne de m'ê - tre trom - pée de sai - son D'a - voir pleu - ré au lieu de sou - rire De m'ê - tre nour - rie d'un â - pre re - gime de re - gret D'a - voir a - ban - don - né l'es - poir au sou - ven - ir Je me par -

B sect:

- don - ne d'a - voir é - tu - dié a - vec tant d'a - char - ne - ment La pous - siére de la route dé - jà par - cou - rue Comme si je sus - ci - te - rais des em - prein - tes d'a - mours fa - nés Une dou - ceur que je n'a - vais jam - ais con - nu, que j'i - gnor - ais Une dou - ceur que je n'a - vais jam - ais con - nu

85

Pathway with a Heart

It was a good book they gave to me
But what's the use if I can't see to turn the pages over?
All those lost dreams of yesterday –
Tears in my eyes make me forget I chose to be a rover.
Not for me the beaten track, no, not the well worn phrases.
I choose a pathway with a heart – no stones to mark the stages.

Another way might look the same;
But there's only pain and an aching soul for those that walk along it,
But mine is a pathway with a heart
Which calls to me and makes me sing whenever I walk upon it.
Not for me the printed word, no gurus and no sages.
I choose a pathway with a heart, no familiar stopping places.

Though each of us is all alone
It's strange that I expect to see you just round every corner.
I let you go and yet I know
The more I do, the more our pathways seem to be coming closer:
Near is far and far is near, no well known destination.
If you choose a pathway with a heart, the goal is your own creation.

Though each of us is all alone
It's strange that I expect to see you just round every corner.
I let you go and yet I know,
The more I do the more our pathways seem to be coming closer... closer... closer.

♩=135 — **A sect:**

| G | | B7 |

It was a good book they gave to me But what's the use if I

| CMaj7 | D | Gadd9 |

... can't see to tu-rn the page-s o-ver All

| G | B7 | CMaj7 |

those lost dreams of yes-terday Tears in my eyes make me for-get I

| D | Gadd9 | **B sect:** B7 | CMaj7 |

cho-se to be a rov-er Not for me the beat-en track,

| CMaj7 | D7 | Gadd9 |

no, not the well worn phra-ses I choose a path-way

| G/B Gadd9 | CMaj7 | D | Gadd9 |

with a heart - no stones to mark the sta-ges An-

87

Pipy's Song

Every day of my life, every moment of the day
I am held in the beauty of our love,
For this love turned the key that has set my spirit free;
It is the fountain of everything I give;
And now my circle of freedom is as big as the world
And as small as the place here where I stand,
And though nothing can shake it and no-one can take it
We share it when I give to you my hand,
And though nothing can shake it and no-one can take it
We share it when I give to you my hand.

When I walk in the forest every tree is a friend
And the roots are the guardians of my dreams,
And if I open my heart wide, then I'll let the sun inside
And every pathway becomes more than what it seems.
And though the trees they may tumble and the branches may fall
I can still feel their blessing coming through.
In my heart they still grow, in my dreams they still show
The pathway that is leading me to you.
In my heart they still grow, in my dreams they still show
The pathway that is leading me to you.

When the streets seem full of strangers and the moments full of pain
And I seem to lose direction in the crowd,
Then the song that we share fills the world with light again
And I find myself singing it aloud;
And there's no need to give out my name to the world,
No need to call attention to my face…
When we meet we shall know, as so often long ago,
That love is the temple of all peace.
When we meet we shall know, as so often long ago,
That love is the temple of all peace.
Love is the temple of all peace.

♩=174

Every day of my life, every moment of the day I am
held in the beauty of our love For this love turned the key
that has set my spirit free 'Tis a fountain of
every-thing I give And now my circle of freedom is as
big as the world And as small as the place here where I stand
And though nothing can shake it and no-one can take it We
share it when I give to you my hand And though nothing can
shake it and no-one can take it We share it when I
give to you my hand When I...

That Fire

I met her in the wintertime as the day began to fall.
She bade me stay awhile and hear the words that she would tell.
She was grey as stone and broken bark; she was withered old and wild,
But the eyes that pierced right to my heart were the clear eyes of a child.
The hems about her garments they were faintly glowing green,
The berries tangled in her hair were the jewels of a queen.
She was innocent as flowers, she was rich as the earth in spring
And the soil itself began to speak when she began to sing.

When you've been the road of loneliness, you've been the road of pain;
When you've felt the drop inside yourself and struggled up again.
When you've learnt to say 'Farewell, adieu', bid those you love good cheer,
There's nowhere to stay but only now, nowhere to be but here.
When the stars have lost their lustre, when a stone is only stone,
When every door seems painted shut and the grass is merely green,
Then bring in the logs and branches, light up the fire within,
For the earth begins to shine again when that fire starts to burn.

When the words can't hold their colours, when they slip out from your hand.
When the dreams that filled your cup with songs have drained into the sand,
When you've learned to bless the emptiness, long furrows bleak and bare,
There's nowhere to stay but only now, nowhere to be but here.
When the stars have lost their lustre, when a stone is only stone,
When every door seems painted shut and the grass is merely green,
Then bring in the logs and branches, light up the fire within,
For the earth begins to shine again when that fire starts to burn.

=140
A sect:
D G D/F♯ D
I ... met her in the win - ter - time as the day be - gan to fall She
G D Bm
bade me stay a - while and hear the words that she would tell
A D G D/F♯
She was grey as stone and bro - ken bark; she was with - ered old and
D G D
wild But the eyes that pierced right to my heart were the
Bm A D
clear eyes of a child
B sect:
G D/F♯
The hems a - bout her gar - ments they were
G D/F♯ G
faint - ly glow - ing green The berries tan - gled
D Bm A D
in her hair were the jew - els of a queen She was in - no - cent as
G D/F♯ D G
flow - ers, she was rich as the earth in spring And the soil it - self be -
D/F♯ Bm A D
gan to speak when she be - gan to sing When you've

I Did Not Leave

I did not leave, I have come inside.
I have not gone, I am still near.
Listen inwards in the silence
To your beating heart, for I am there.

In the cornfield where the hare runs,
When the swifts have already flown,
In the stillness between the ash trees,
I am here; you are not alone.
Chorus

When you release the strings that bind us,
When you let my soul go free,
And I know I'm not forgotten
Then the love flows easily.
Chorus

Do not seek me at the graveside,
You will not find me on the earth,
But the dragonfly darting between us
Tells not of endings, this is my birth.
Chorus

And when a song rises inside you,
Whenever the dancing takes your feet,
When all the lonely pathways gather
Then I'll be with you when you meet.
Chorus

And when your road is barred with shadows,
And the clouds are a maze of grey,
Then all my longing is to work with you
And if you call we shall find the way.
Chorus

When autumn light lies on the meadows,
When winter light gleams on the hill,
When spring is young in every garden
And summer eves are sweet and still.
Chorus

Dedicated to Richard, Judy and Lawrence

♩=145 **A sect:**

I did not leave, I have come in-side I have not gone,

I am still near Listen in-wards in the sil-ence To your beat-ing

B sect:

heart, for I am there In the corn field

where the hare runs When the swifts have al-rea-dy flown

In the still-ness be-tween the ash trees I am here; you are

not a-lone For I did not

Jehanne Mehta accompanied the founding group of the Gatekeeper Trust in the early 1980s, inspired to walk along ancient pathways of England in pilgrimage with an awareness of the sacred nature of our environment. She contributed her creative inspiration and love of the Earth through song.

Gatekeeper Trust

Albion

This Place

This place is ancient, a place where the roads meet,
Showing lines in the landscape that were laid down by stars.
The wisdom the earth has been holding in secret
Begins to be known again as the years pass,
Begins to be known again as the years pass.

This place is ancient, a place where the trees grew;
The groves of great yew trees and later of oak,
Where creation was honoured by the old ones, the wise ones
And this place still remembers the words that they spoke,
And this place still remembers the words that they spoke.

This place is ancient: great stones mark the sunrise,
The moonrise and star-rise, the cycles of time,
Where the land holds the key to the wide cosmic dance
And we learn where we came from and how to return,
And we learn where we came from and how to return.

This place is ancient, a place of high power,
With roots that lie deeper than ever were seen;
On the one hand stands love, on the other stands wisdom,
And the gateway to Albion lies in between,
And the gateway to Albion lies in between.

But this place here is new, it is under construction —
Far stronger than stone is the love that we share.
This place is inward. It points to the future.
This place is a temple because we meet here,
This place is a temple because we meet here.

♩=129

This place is an-cient, a place where the roads meet Show-ing lines in the land-scape that were laid down by stars The wis-dom the earth has been hold-ing in sec-ret Be-gins to be known a-gain as the years pass Be-gins to be known a-gain as the years pass

Song of the Fosterer

Oh the lark in the morning she springs from her nest
And she soars to the clouds with the dawn on her breast,
But e'er she has risen you must be away
With wings on your heels you must conquer the day.
Learn to climb like a squirrel and spring like the hare
And to run like the hounds in pursuit of the deer,
To juggle with language and master the word
And then you'll be fitted to handle a sword.

When first you came to me but late from the breast,
Like an unfledged cock linnet cast out from the nest,
Like a treasure fished up from the depths of the weir,
None thought I so precious, nor none held so dear.
There was no time to waste for your life had begun,
Oh how swiftly you grew in the light of the sun,
With the wild wood to teach you and the song of the bird,
And soon you'll be fitted to handle a sword.

The swoop of the hawk as it falls through the air,
The stealth of the fox as he creeps to his lair,
You can hear every movement and read every sound,
Sharp eared as the hare in her form on the ground.
And tales I have told you of heroes of old,
Of slaying of dragons and treasures of gold,
Of creation and magic and myth you have heard
And soon you'll be fitted to handle a sword.

How small you were still when I taught you to swim,
Scarce firm on your feet but I tumbled you in.
Now you slide through the water with the grace of an eel,
When the salmon's away you are close on his tail.
And straight you have grown like a sapling and long,
As limber as willow, as tough and as strong.
The growing is easy but the learning is hard
And soon you'll be fitted to handle a sword.

[continued overleaf]

♩=150　A sect:

Oh the lark in the mor - ning she springs from her nest And she
soars to the clouds with the dawn on her breast But e're she has
ris - en you must be a - way With wings on your heels you must
con - quer the day:　B sect: Learn to climb like a squir - rel and
spring like the hare And to run like the hounds in pur - suit of the deer
To jug - gle with lang - uage and mas - ter the word
　　　　　　　　　　　　　　　　　　　　　　　　　　Violin:
And then you'll be fit - ed to han - dle a sword
　　　　　　　　　　　　　　　　　　　　Voice:
(When...)

99

In the dusk of the forest and the tumbling stream
Your clear eyes can see all there is to be seen,
The shadows of birds in the dun coloured shade,
The sway of a fish in the flickering green.
And music is yours for I taught you to play
The soft notes of the harp to enliven the day,
In time you will master the songs of the bard,
But now you are fitted to handle a sword,
Now you are fitted to handle a sword.

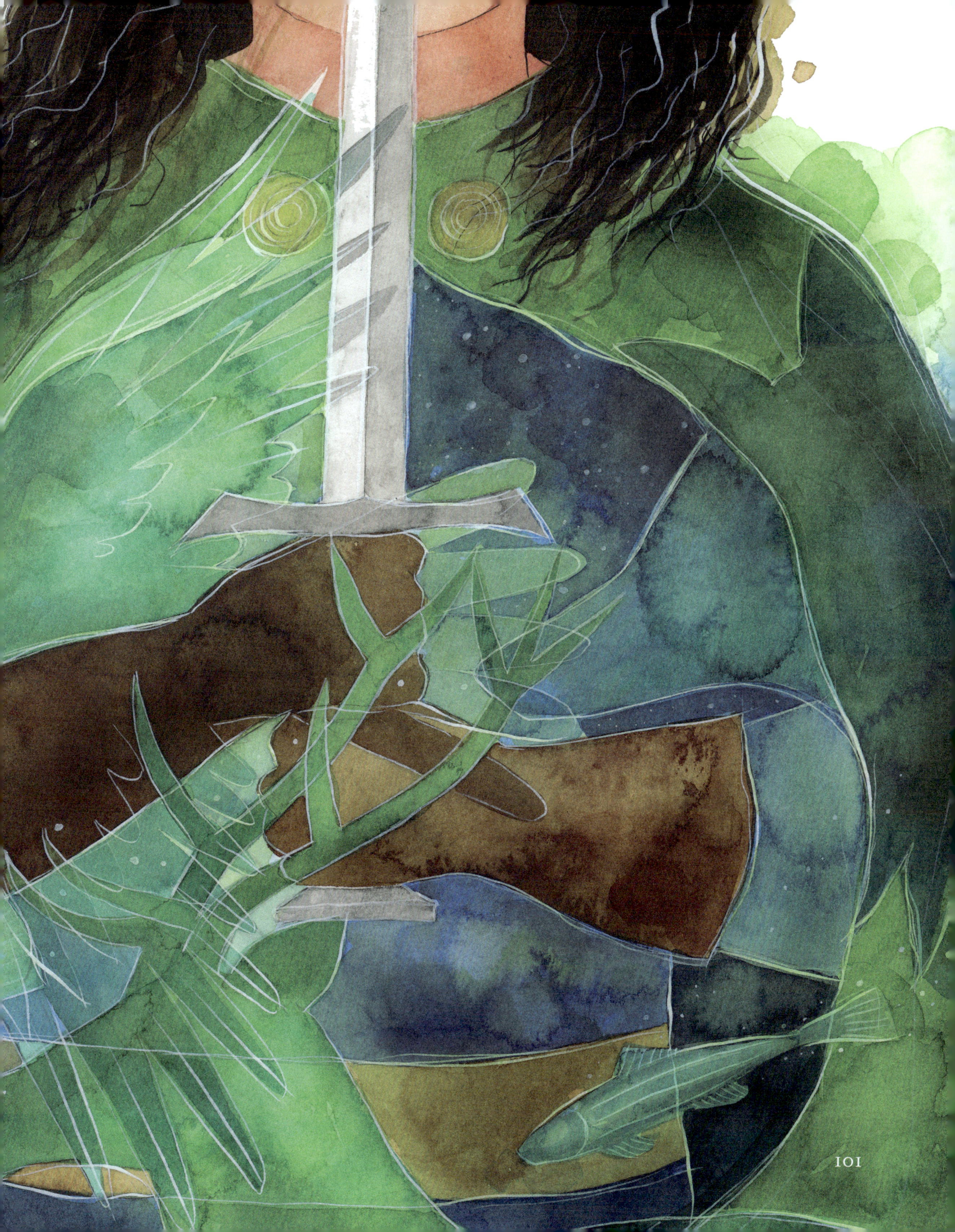

Song Hunt

I'm away this bright morning to hunt for a song: the hunting I hope will be good.
I've no firm idea which direction to take – over heathland or into the wood.
My quarry's elusive, not easy to spot even when hounds have picked up the scent.
'Twill appear just as clear as the moon on a hill then 'tis gone with no clue where it went.

Tally-ho, hark away, the morning is fair
Hark away tally-ho hark away.

In your fox hunt bold Reynard will use all his skill and will oft double back on his tracks
And while hounds are thrashing around for the scent he'll be slinking by close to their backs.
But in this kind of hunt you must call in your hounds and keep them quite still at your heel,
Then your quarry will boldly come half-way to meet you and hounds may surround it at will.
Chorus

If I think I have any idea what to look for I know I am wasting my time.
Every fox has two sharp pointed ears and a brush, but no two songs are ever the same.
As I ride o'er the hill on a fine winter's morn with the grass showing green through the snow,
My quarry so lightly is running beside; I can hear the wind telling me so.
Chorus

So I turn in the saddle and glimpse a dim shape and I sound the shrill notes of my horn
And the hounds scurry round to follow the scent, but my quarry has vanished and gone.
Did it take to the water or take to the air? Is it hounds that I need or a gun?
Perplexed I draw rein to define a fresh aim as I watch the good hounds in the sun.
Chorus

'Here Dinah, here Messenger, Sunny and Frey, think we'll call off the hunt for today.
We've hunted too hard and we've made too much noise and our quarry's been frightened away.'
So despondent and weary I sit down to rest before crossing the hills to go home,
When calm from the brushwood my quarry appears. Now tell me, did I catch my song?
Chorus

♩.=88 [A sect:]

I'm a-way this bright mor-ning to hunt for a song The hunt-ing I hope will be

good I've no firm i-dea which di-rec-tion to take Ov-er

heath-land or in-to the wood My quar-ry's el-u-sive not

eas-y to spot Ev-en when hounds have picked up the scent 'Twill ap-

pear just as clear as the moon on a hill Then 'tis gone with no clue where it

[B sect:]

went Tal-ly-ho, hark a-way the mor-ning is fair Hark a-

way tal-ly-ho hark a-way (In your

The Slow Motion Waltz

On a midsummer's evening when the sun it goes down then it's time to creep out on the trail;
Oh shall we go flirting from under the skirting and join the invertebrates' ball?
Let us gracefully twine in our silvery slime, how the melody quickens my pulse!
How could it be wrong to go sliming along to the strains of the slow motion waltz,
How could it be wrong to go sliming along to the strains of the slow motion waltz?

With your sleek black antennae as bright as a penny you're sure to be belle of the ball,
And how all will admire your shiny attire and the elegant point of your tail.
So come on my dear, let us join in the cheer, your modesty strikes me as false,
How could it be wrong to go sliming along to the strains of the slow motion waltz?
How could it be wrong to go sliming along to the strains of the slow motion waltz?

She replies:

If you were to invite me for a turn round the garden to sample a cabbage or two,
Oh how glad I would be to go out on the spree: just me and the moonlight and you.
But a terrible fear bids me hold back my dear; nothing personal, dearest of course,
But what dangers may lurk way out there in the murk if we join in the slow motion waltz,
But what dangers may lurk way out there in the murk if we join in the slow motion waltz?

You see my dear brother Wilberforce crept out one day for a turn round the cornflakes and tea,
With a ring in his ear and his tiger stripe gear, oh how foolish and headstrong was he.
He was fearless, but ah there was no lid on the jar and he'd climbed right on top of the rim,
He hadn't a hope for he slipped down the slope to slow death in the red currant jam.
He hadn't a hope for he slipped down the slope to slow death in the red currant jam.

But he is not to be deterred.

Come, come my dear lassie, life's full of such dangers and sooner or later we die;
We must not with impunity flout opportunity staring us straight in the eye.
Let us slither and slide while our trails side by side meander o'er cupboards and floors,
How could it be wrong to go sliming along to the strains of the slow motion waltz?
How could it be wrong to go sliming along to the strains of the slow motion waltz?

(A love song for slugs, which are actually hermaphrodite)

♩=154

C On a mid-sum-mer's eve-ning when the sun it goes down then it's **F**

G time to creep out on the trail **C G C** Oh shall we go flirt-ing from un-der the **F**

F G skirt-ing And join the in-vert-e-brates' ball **C** Let us grace-ful-ly twine in our sil-ver-y **F**

F C slime How the mel-o-dy quick-ens my pulse **G C** How could it be wrong to go slim-ing a- **F**

F G long To the strains of the slow mo-tion waltz **C G C** How could it be wrong to go slim-ing a- **F**

F G long To the strains of the slow mo-tion waltz **C G** (With your)

River Man

Oh there was an old man and he lived on the hill
And he had one lovely daughter.
All along by the riverside she would roam,
All along by the flowing water.
And it's 'Stay pretty daughter, stay at home
And take good care of your daddy,
And you shall be wed to handsome Billy Jones
And he'll make you a bonny little lady.'

'Oh handsome Billy Jones he can leave me alone
With his neat little home on the corner
And I never want to be anybody's Mrs Jones
With a colour television and a freezer,
Where the music is canned and the weeds are all banned
And your thoughts are all folded and tidy,
For I've fallen in love with the river' she said,
'And I'll go where the river song calls me.'

So she's tangled the marigolds in her hair
And she's called farewell to her daddy.
On the kingfisher's path she has rambled away
All under the wild white cherry.
And tall as a tree the river man stood,
And he sparkled with blue green laughter,
'Let us hasten away on the shimmering wave,
While the wind comes a-following after.'

So he's gathered her up in his berry brown arms
And they sang as they went through the water,
And never could I find where the river man dwells
With the old man's beautiful daughter;
But I walked by the river and I lingered awhile
And I heard their children calling:
The dipper and the dabchick and the little wagtail
Where they played by the banks in the morning.

O there was an old man and he lived on the hill And he had one love-ly daugh-ter All a-long by the riv-er-side she would roam All a-long by the flow-ing wa-ter And it's 'Stay pret-ty daugh-ter, stay at home And take good care of your dad-dy And you shall be wed to hand-some Bil-ly Jones And he'll make you a bon-ny lit-tle la-dy'

Dulcimer:

The Rollright Stones

Come all you folk that like to hear old stories told in song,
Lend me your ears a little while; I'll not detain you long;
'Tis not of love or soldiery, of toil nor yet of trade,
But such tales as down the years are into myth and legend made,
But such tales as down the years are into myth and legend made.

A king there came from far away his fortune for to win,
To see if he were fitted to be all England's king,
And high upon the Cotswold ridge there stood an ancient crone,
She was keeper of the mysteries of wood and earth and stone. *Repeat*

'Sir King do not come lightly into this sacred place,
If kingship be to win here there be dangers thou must face,
And seven lengthy strides thou must now learn to take,
That thou mayst know the ancient lore, or kingship else forsake. *Repeat*

For kingship is not like the chase, it is a sacred trust,
For thou must love and hold the land and give her of thy best.
In high times as in hollow times, in times both fair and ill,
Be keeper of the mysteries of wildwood, grove and hill.' *Repeat*

The king he made him ready but he was quick and proud.
E'er six steps he had taken, he shouted out aloud,
He shouted with a mighty voice, 'By stick, by stock and stone,
As high king of all fair England I shall e'er long be known.' *Repeat*

Straightway before his eyes it seemed a mound of earth there was,
And as from out the darkness, he heard the fearsome voice,
'The secrets of the ancient lore thou mayst not now behold,
For thy pride has brought thy downfall, as stone thou shalt be held.' *Repeat*

As stone the king now sleeps and as stone all of his men,
A-waiting to be woken that he may try again,
The seven strides to take and the vision for to win,
Whereby he may be fitted to be all England's king. *Repeat*

♩=143 *a capella*

Come all you folk who like to hear old stor-ies told in song
Lend me your ears a lit-tle while; I'll not de-tain you long
'Tis not of love or sol-dier-y, of toil nor yet of trade
But such tales as down the years are in-to myth and le-gend made
But such tales as down the years are in-to myth and le-gend made

Long centuries have rolled away since these things came to pass;
All in a ring the weathered stones still lean out of the grass.
To learn again Earth's mysteries the choice is ours to make:
Like a stone to sleep the changes through, or else to stir and wake. *Repeat*

Based on the legend of the King's Men (the circle of stones at Rollright), the King Stone and the Witch of Long Compton.

Edward

In Gloucester city there lies a king.
Fair he is above anything.
Around his stone head the curls hang down,
Under the burden of his crown.
'Edward my name and here my tomb.
Brutal my ending in Berkeley's gloom,
But lend me a moment and I will speak with you;

For you have life and you have breath,
I've been too long a prisoner of my death.
O give me a chance and let me dance with you,
O give me a chance and let me dance with you.

The scabious blooms on the golden hill.
The grasshopper scrapes in the burnet still
When the wagoner's gone and the acre is bare
And the thatcher has gathered his roofing straw.
I could thatch you a roof, I loved ditching and walling,
Though 'twas scarcely considered a kingly calling,
And wherever you toil there let me toil with you; *Chorus*

Music I loved and minstrelsy,
The pipe and the tabor and psaltery
And Roger the crwthier played for me,
From the mountains of Wales by the western sea,
And Richard the rhymer at fair Langley
Did sing for our court and our company,
And wherever you sing there let me sing with you; *Chorus*

Where are the players in mask and gown
Who gather the crowds in the market town?
There's many a story in tumble and turn.
What folly can fools from the wise man learn.
Pretenders by laughter are put to the test
By the clown with his cap, his bell and his jest
And wherever you laugh there let me laugh with you; *Chorus*

Here on Severn's fair eastern shore
Is the tomb where I will lie no more.
My fault if truly you count it one
Was loving young Peter of Gaveston,
But love is a blossom without compare.
Wherever it grows then tend it there
And wherever you love there let me love with you;'
Chorus

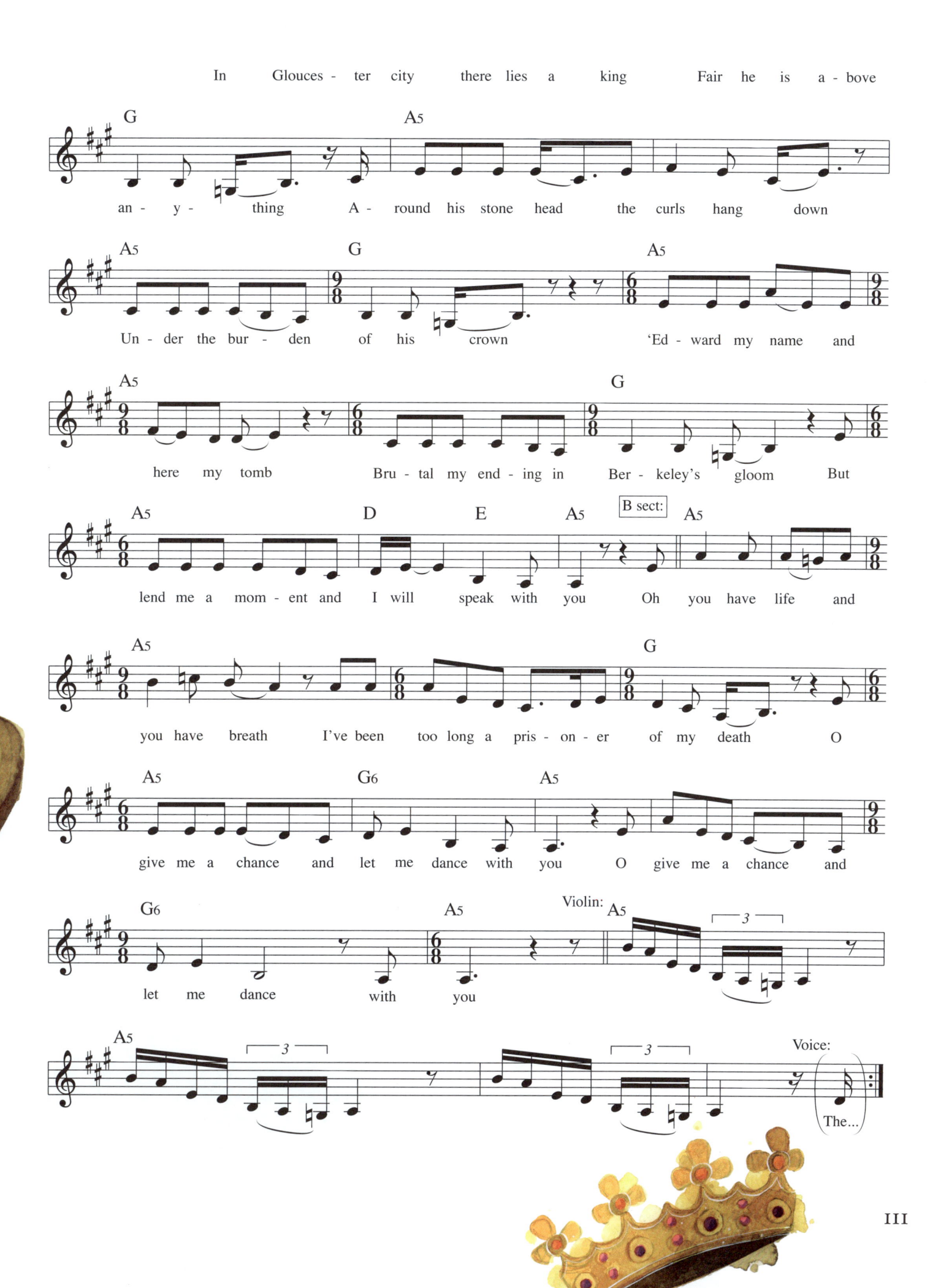

In Glouces-ter city there lies a king Fair he is a-bove an-y-thing A-round his stone head the curls hang down Un-der the bur-den of his crown 'Ed-ward my name and here my tomb Bru-tal my end-ing in Ber-keley's gloom But lend me a mom-ent and I will speak with you Oh you have life and you have breath I've been too long a pris-on-er of my death O give me a chance and let me dance with you O give me a chance and let me dance with you

Violin:

Voice: The...

The Fields of Runnymede

Where the river swings in channels wide
Past Windsor walls in stately tide
Where the bittern calls and the wild ducks glide
Through rush and sedge and reed
Here lie the fields of high renown
Where the Thames rolls by to London town
And wisdom springs in sacred ground
The fields of Runnymede

Oh braided in like beads of green
Here islands float with the tide between
With willows silver glistening
By rush and sedge and reed
And one of these a place I know
Where those who seek deep silence go
And roots reach down to long ago
In the fields of Runnymede

There stands a tree but more than tree
Beneath a dusky canopy
The home of runes and mystery
By rush and sedge and reed
And those who would true counsel seek
From far and near their journey make
To the ancient yew of Ankerwyke
In the fields of Runnymede

To the ground where grows this hallowed tree
Many hundred years a sanctuary
May come no trace of treachery
By rush and sedge and reed
'Tis a fitting place for the oath swearing
When the barons bold press John the King
To uphold the rights of all free men
In the fields of Runnymede

So the barons of all England came
With little trust but sure of aim
The powers of the king to tame
By rush and sedge and reed
There is higher law than royal will
To the Charter John must set his seal
And to earth new seeds of freedom fell
In the fields of Runnymede

Though islands float in the Thames no more
And ceaseless streams of traffic roar
Yet there remains a place of awe
By rush and sedge and reed
It is earth's healing now we seek
From the roots of wisdom let him speak
Oh sacred yew of Ankerwyke
In the fields of Runnymede

♩=63 *a capella*
Rubato

Where the riv-er swings in chan-nels wide Past
Wind-sor walls in state-ly tide Where the
bit-tern calls and the wild ducks glide Through
rush and sedge and reed Here lie the fields of high re-nown Where the
Thames rolls by to Lon-don town And wis-dom springs in sac-red ground The
fi-elds of Run-ny-mede (Oh)

The Greenway

There is life in your feet when you walk on the greenway;
You can dance up the flowers and re-grow the trees,
And the pulse of the soil feels the beat of your dancing,
And the flows of the earth feel the warmth of your feet.

Will you walk on the greenway, walk on the greenway,
Walk on the greenway with me, walk on the greenway with me?

There is life in your hands when you walk on the greenway;
At your touch feel the stirring of sap in the stones,
Feel the trees pulling free to peer over your shoulder
And the fields of the air spreading widening wings. *Chorus*

There is life in your heart when you walk on the greenway.
The high hopes of so many heartways meet here.
No haven is far and no pain is unending;
The shimmer of jewels inside every tear. *Chorus*

Oh music and the greenway are never far parted:
The tumble of torrents the rustle of spray,
And the voices of streamlets in bubbles and trebles
Fill the mornings with laughter all down to the sea. *Chorus*

For someone is emerging when you walk on the greenway,
A widening smile ripples into the air.
Feel the tingle of shoots reaching out from your fingers,
Unfurling of delicate leaves in your hair. *Chorus*

For the changes begin when you walk on the greenway,
The roots reconnect with the sky and the stars,
And your heart is the ear that is tuned to the earth's way
And you are the song she is listening for. *Chorus*

=145
A sect:
Gm F Gm
There is life in your feet when you walk on the green - way You can
Gm F Gm
dance up the flow - ers and re - grow the trees And the pulse of the soil
F Gm
feels the beat of your danc - ing And the flows of the earth feel the
Gm Dm7 B sect: B♭ F E♭
warmth of your feet Will you walk on the green way; walk on the
Gm F E♭
green - way Walk on the green - way with me
E♭ F Gm
walk on the green - way with me There is

The Metal Worker's Apprentice

Oh the old woods can tell you the story's beginning
Of coppicing stands of young beech wood and oak
And the smoky faced colliers who stacked up the kilns
For slow burning of charcoal the fires for to stoke;
While the smith he stood by with his apron and tongs
To heat up the iron until it glowed white
For forging the tools and the knives for our use
And to wield his old hammer it was his delight.

Sing copper, bronze and mercury, silver lead and tin
And a bunch of bright planets to range them all in.
There's Venus, Mars and Jupiter, Saturn and the moon
With your iron on the anvil and gold like the sun.

Now it's time once again to take up the old skills
Of forging and casting until you know how,
Apprenticed to metals and all kinds of labour,
It's tough and it's toil but you learn as you go;
And whatever the task it comes down to the rhythm,
The beat of your heart and the tides of your breath,
Swinging your arm as you handle the hammer,
Shaping the metals from under the earth. *Chorus*

It takes fire to soften an ingot of silver
And beat it in rhythm until the form's clear,
For your spoon and your fork watch the shape like a hawk
While the clink of your hammers is music to hear:
And then comes the bowling, the buffing and polishing
'Till you can see yourself mirrored inside
And at last all your work it is finished and ready
To set on fine linen with candles beside. *Chorus*

[continued overleaf]

♩=150 **A sect:**

Oh the old woods can tell you the story's beginning Of coppicing stands of young beach wood and oak And the smoky faced colliers who stacked up the kilns For slow burning of charcoal the fires for to stoke; While the smith he stood by with his apron and tongs To heat up the iron until it glowed white For forging the tools and the knives for our use And to wield his old hammer it was his delight

Violin:

B sect: *a capella Rubato*

Sing.... copper, bronze and mercury, silver, lead and

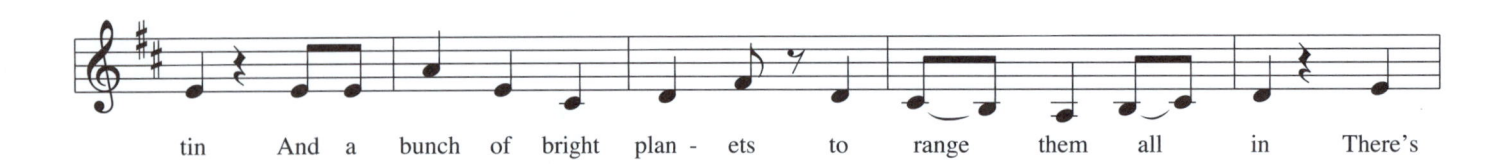

...tin And a bunch of bright planets to range them all in There's Venus, Mars and Jupiter, Saturn and the moon With your iron on the anvil and gold like the sun (Now it's...

Now the pewterer's craft it goes back through the ages
For turning your goblet and chalice and bowl,
Never forgetting the candlestick maker
To lay the long table for a feast of goodwill.
So let's keep alive the old skills and traditions,
As we learn how to cast and to draft and to spin,
Making tankards and chessmen and vases of beauty
To show the soft gleam and the shine of the tin. *Chorus*

Oh long is the story of the king of all metals.
With fever and toil it came out of the earth,
But for gilding of icons and art you need only
Your skill with gold leaf that'll float on your breath;
And finest among all the uses of gold
Is a craft of the alchemist, making of balm,
Mixing the powder with beeswax and rose,
To bring back to your centre the warmth of the sun. *Chorus*

Commissioned for Freeman College Sheffield, by Aonghus Gordon

119

Her work is full of the magic and mystery of the ancient ballads, but still speaks with a contemporary voice, timeless and relevant, and committed to current issues.

John Kirkpatrick, musician

Myth & Legend

Arthur the King

Brave Arthur was buried, so legends they tell it,
Deep under the mountains in days long ago,
With twelve faithful knights decked in armour like silver,
With their long swords beside them in scabbards of gold;
But dying is only a new kind of waking,
Or a new kind of sleeping, resplendent with dream.
'If times they are hard you have only to call me,
And you'll not catch me napping', said Arthur the King.

So we'll kindle a beacon on every high mountain, to the sound of our music the valleys shall ring,
To waken the sleepers of long vanished ages, to waken the knights and brave Arthur the King.

Well the dragon may prowl in the streets of the city
And the world may turn out to be not what it seems,
And many a job may be axed by tomorrow
And we may be obliged to abandon our dreams,
But bring in the fool in his motley and bells
And remember the minstrels who taught you to sing
And the quest it begins with the steps of the dance,
'Won't you please find your partners?', said Arthur the King. *Chorus*

There's no need to seek far to find news of disaster,
Of wars and of rumours of gathering gloom,
And it's hard to escape the dead weight of inertia
As we hear the fraught words of the prophets of doom;
But each knight is equal around my round table
And each has a note and a rhythm to bring,
And the quest it begins with the jig and the reel,
'Won't you take out your fiddles?', said Arthur the King. *Chorus*

There are times when the fog is so thick on the hills,
Fell enchantments have settled on river and lake,
And the poisons have sunk so far into the Earth
That we ask is there anything left there to wake;
But bring in the Morris, the sword dance and step dance;
The music is there and you know how to sing,
And the quest it begins with the song from the heart,
'Won't you join in the chorus?', said Arthur the King. *Chorus*

♩=148 | **A sect:**

Brave Arthur was buried, so legends they tell it Deep under the mountains in days long ago With twelve faithful knights decked in armour like silver With their long swords beside them in scabbards of gold 'But dying is only a new kind of waking Or a new kind of sleeping resplendent with dream (And) if times they are hard you have only to call me and you'll not catch me napping' said Arthur the King

B sect:

So we'll kindle a beacon on every high mountain To the sound of our music the valeys shall ring To waken the sleepers of long van--ished a-ges To welcome the knights and brave Arthur the King

Violin: ... Voice: Well the...

La Belle Dormant

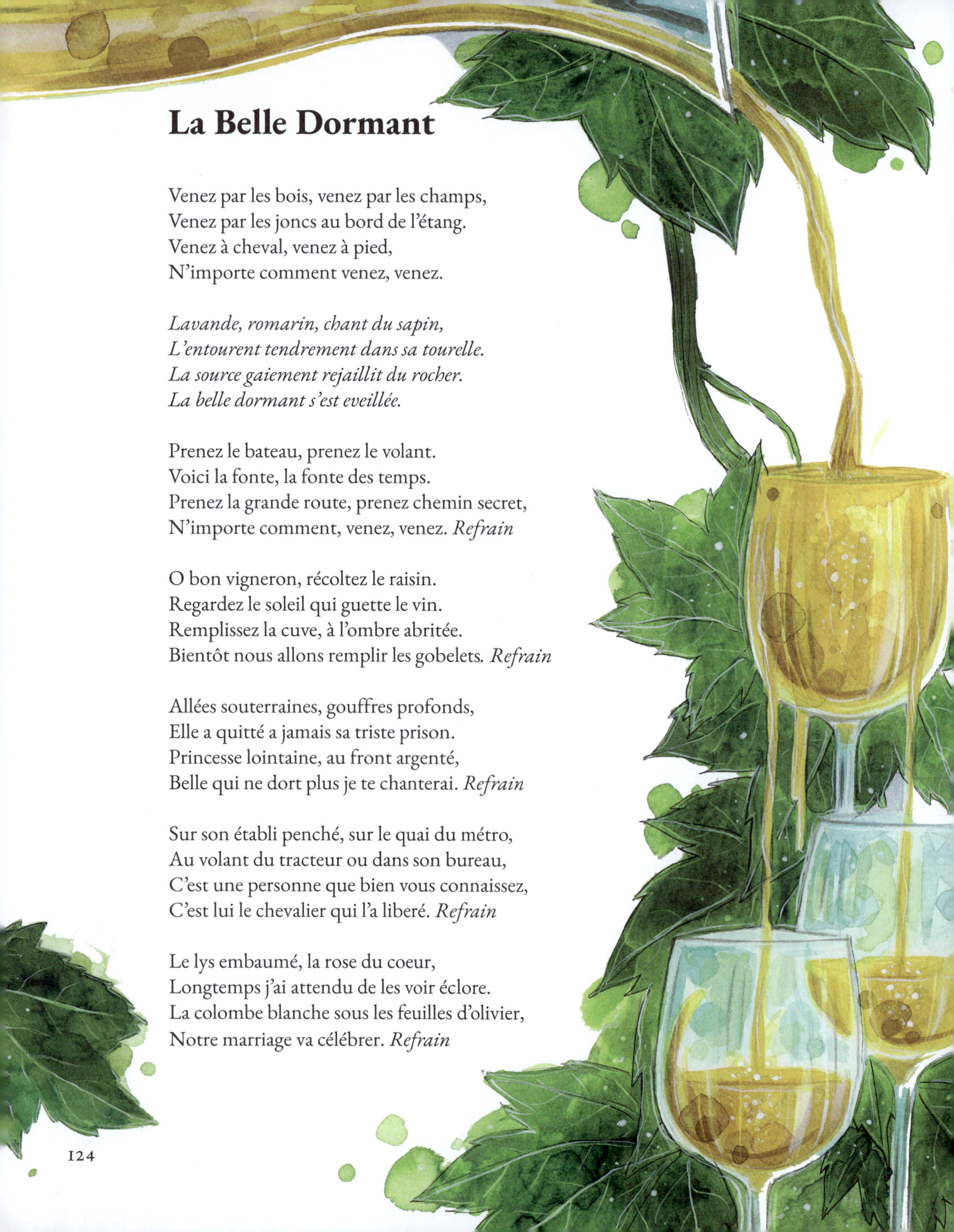

Venez par les bois, venez par les champs,
Venez par les joncs au bord de l'étang.
Venez à cheval, venez à pied,
N'importe comment venez, venez.

Lavande, romarin, chant du sapin,
L'entourent tendrement dans sa tourelle.
La source gaiement rejaillit du rocher.
La belle dormant s'est eveillée.

Prenez le bateau, prenez le volant.
Voici la fonte, la fonte des temps.
Prenez la grande route, prenez chemin secret,
N'importe comment, venez, venez. *Refrain*

O bon vigneron, récoltez le raisin.
Regardez le soleil qui guette le vin.
Remplissez la cuve, à l'ombre abritée.
Bientôt nous allons remplir les gobelets. *Refrain*

Allées souterraines, gouffres profonds,
Elle a quitté a jamais sa triste prison.
Princesse lointaine, au front argenté,
Belle qui ne dort plus je te chanterai. *Refrain*

Sur son établi penché, sur le quai du métro,
Au volant du tracteur ou dans son bureau,
C'est une personne que bien vous connaissez,
C'est lui le chevalier qui l'a liberé. *Refrain*

Le lys embaumé, la rose du coeur,
Longtemps j'ai attendu de les voir éclore.
La colombe blanche sous les feuilles d'olivier,
Notre marriage va célébrer. *Refrain*

♩=142 A sect:

Venez par les bois, venez par les champs Venez par les joncs au bord de l'é-tang Venez à che-val, venez à pied N'im-por-te com-ment venez, venez La-

B sect:

vande, ro-marin chant du sa-pin L'en-tour-ent ten-dre-ment dans sa tour-el-le La source gaie-ment re-jail-lit du ro-cher La belle dor-ment s'est ev-eil-lé

Mandolin:

The Fountain

I'll tell to you a tale of love that once to me befell.
I thought that I was proof against that sweet and thorny spell,
But little did I know the art that day I was to see.
He master was of changing shapes and all love's mystery.

Across the vale at Lammas tide he came with graceful stride,
And I was taken by surprise and found no place to hide.
I went out on the broad hillside and there began to run,
But when I looked behind I knew that race was scarce begun.

My love became a good greyhound upon the open field.
He chased me over moor and dale and forcèd me to yield.
I ran unto the river's brim and quickly plungèd in,
But when I looked behind I knew that race I could not win.

My love became a golden fish that swims against the tide,
And every turn that I would make he swam along beside.
Then I became a little bird that flies into the wind
But when I looked around I saw he was not far behind.

For carried by the singing wind that blows upon the hill,
My love became a falcon swift that swoops upon the kill.
Then he became an errant knight and swordplay was his art,
And he drew out his golden blade and pierced me to the heart.

The leaves fall softly on the ground this grey October morn.
Like drops of blood the berries are that grow upon the thorn.
Like drops of blood that from my heart are falling on the ground.
Although I'm pierced right to the quick, I would not make a sound.

O down in yonder garden green there flows a fountain clear,
Where I may drink the crystal drops and wash away my tears.
For love is like a fountainhead of sharp and bitter birth.
Although it fills the heart with pain it waters all the earth.

♩=137 **A sect:**

I'll tell to you a tale of love That once to me be-fell

I thought that I was proof a-gainst that

sweet and thorn-y spell **B sect:** But lit-tle did I know the art That

day I was to see He mas-ter was of

chang-ing shapes and all love's mys-ter-y

A-cross...

Basket of Roses

Here comes a knight riding over the hill to rescue the king's fair daughter
'And what have you got to maintain her on, and what have you brought to win her?'
'I have brought her silver, brought her gold and a pearl from the floor of the ocean.
And love I have brought to maintain her on wrapped up in a basket of roses.'

Here comes a knight riding over the hill to rescue the king's fair daughter.
'And how will you pierce the walls of stone, and what will you do to wake her?'
'I have winds from the east, north, south and west and a sword from under the water;
And music to topple the walls of stone and the notes of a song to wake her.'

So he's hewed to the left and he's hewed to the right and he's cut him a path through the bramble
But there's never a scratch on his berry brown skin, in his gold hair never a tangle.
In his stirrups he rose and he whistled the winds from their home in the bleak of the ocean,
And the sound of the storm made the hills to resound and set all the branches in motion.

Quite still he sat till he took out his harp in the midst of the murk and commotion,
And his fingers went rippling over the strings and the tune was much sweeter than honey.
And behold 'twas a terrible sight to see how the mountain began for to tremble
And stone after stone from the ramparts fell and the walls in the dust did crumble.

Then into the hall rode this knight of the harp ere the dust on the floor could settle,
And the song that he sang made the rafters to ring and awakened the king's fair daughter.
He has brought her silver, brought her gold and a pearl from the ocean's prizes,
But more precious by far is the gift she will find, wrapped up in the basket of roses;
More precious by far is the gift she will find, wrapped up in the basket of roses.

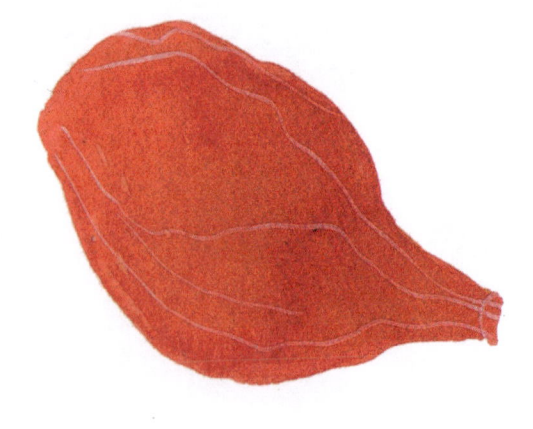

♩=147 **A sect:**

Here comes a knight riding over the hill To rescue the king's fair daughter 'And what have you got to maintain her on And what have you brought to win her?' **B sect:** 'I have brought her silver, brought her gold And a pearl from the floor of the ocean And love I have brought to maintain her on Wrapped up in a basket of roses'

Mandolin:

The Bunch of Keys

Doorways, gateways there to find
Into the world or into the mind,
Into the space at the back of the wind,
And all you need is a bunch of keys.

O the king he would a-hunting go
In the tall bare trees before the snow,
Where the deer and the little red foxes go,
And a bunch of keys he gave to me,

Saying 'Take them, take them, use them well.
You may go wherever you will.
There are treasures aplenty, look your fill,
But this little key, pray leave it be.'

There were doors in the courtyard, doors in the hall,
Doors in the tower and doors in the wall
And a bunch of keys to unlock them all,
All the wonders of the world before me.

Moon and star and beast and tree,
Gold and silver and ivory,
And the sun in the finest dawn array,
And all I did delight to see.

But one little key lies in my hand.
Before the smallest door I stand,
And shall I break the king's command?
What evil curse will fall on me?

I saw your face before I fell,
Down through the darkness, down through the well,
Down to the deepest roots of hell,
And the fiends of hell to greet me.

Down in the silos, deep in the mine,
Down in the nuclear submarine,
I wait for your golden face to shine.
O hear my call and come to me.

The sky is bleak and the sky is grey,
The dull, dead roar of a working day,
But if I turn quickly there I see
A gleam of sunlight beckons me.

I'll share my house, I'll share my all,
I will not heed old Mammon's call
For I don't need any goods at all.
Just as I am I'll follow thee.

Doorways, gateways there to find
Into the world or into the mind
Into the space at the back of the wind,
And all you need is a bunch of keys.

Oh the king he would a-hunting go
In the tall bare trees before the snow,
Where the deer and the little red foxes go,
And a bunch of keys he gave to me.

♩=150

Dm — Door-ways, gate-ways there to find **C** In-to the world or in to the mind

Dm In - to the space at the back of the wind **Am** And

Dm all you need **C** is a **G** bunch of **Dm** keys (Oh the

131

Jean Soleil

Jean Soleil est tout simple
Dans les foules du monde il se perd
Tu le reconnaîtras seulement
Par son regard tout droit
La chaleur de sa voix
La clarté d'un visage ouvert
La clarté d'un visage ouvert

Jean Soleil t'appelle du sommeil
Jean Soleil, Jean Soleil

Jean Soleil sème la paix
Partout où il pose son pied
Tu le reconnaîtras seulement
Par l'étrange silence, par la douce présence
Dans les rues où il vient de passer
Dans les rues où il vient de passer

Jean Soleil donne son pain
Aux oiseaux qui parcourent le ciel
Tu le reconnaîtras seulement,
Par l'absence de peur
Et les flots de son coeur
Qui coule comme le lait et le miel
Qui coule comme le lait et le miel

Jean Soleil tient un secret profond
Caché au creux de sa main
Tu reconnaîtras qu'il est proche
Par la fine plume blanche
Se faufilant dans les branches
Qui vient se poser sur ton chemin

Au milieu de la vie il attend
Derrière la surface du jour
Tout silencieux et sans impatience
Que brille ton coeur
Chassant les ombres de la peur
En allumant les rayons de l'amour
En allumant les rayons de l'amour

Lorsque tu reconnais
Ton pouvoir de tout transformer
Jean Soleil ouvrira les mains
Dans le geste d'une fleur
Se parant de ses plus belles couleurs
Car c'est toi qui est son secret
Car toi, tu est son secret.

Jean Soleil nous appelle du sommeil
Jean Soleil, Jean Soleil.

♩=150 **A sect:**

Jean Soleil est tout simple Dans les foules du monde il se perd
Tu le reconnaîtras seulement Par son re-
gard tout droit La chaleur de sa voix La clarté d'un vis-
a-age ouvert La clarté d'un vis-a-age ouvert

B sect:

Jean Soleil t'appelle du sommeil Jean Soleil...
Jean Soleil Jean Soleil t'appelle du sommeil Jean Soleil... Jean

The Three Sillies

The young man was come to woo: 'Dear daughter, go fetch some beer.'
No matter how long they did wait 'twas in vain, the daughter did never appear.
The old woman she went down the stair: 'Dear daughter, what ails you?' she said.
'O Mother, just see the great axe in the beam, What if it should fall on my head?'

And it's Oh such a silly, my word such a silly, I never did see such a silly before.
If ever I find three such sillies again, I'll come back your daughter to wed.

The old man he went down the stair: 'O tell me what ails you,' he said
'O husband just see the great axe in the beam! it might fall on our dear daughter's head.'
The young man he went down the stair. In amazement he stood by the door:
Mother, father and daughter sat bitterly weeping and the beer ran all over the floor. *Chorus*

The young man soon pulled out the axe and laid it down on the floor.
'I'm off to find three more foolish than you before I return to your door.'
He had not been travelling long when a large pile of walnuts he spied
And a man with a fork trying to load up his wagon and oh, how he fretted and sighed. *Chorus*

'Why not take a basket,' the young man he said, 'to load the nuts onto your cart?'
'Why I ne'er thought of that, good thanks to you Sir! For now I'll be home before dark.'
The oak trees were laden with fruit. A man with a pig he did see:
His face it was red with trying in vain to make his pig climb up the tree. *Chorus*

The young man took hold of a branch. 'Why not shake down the acorns?' said he.
The farmer said 'How did you come by such wits? Such a clever young man as you be.'
'Twas early the following morn; a strange vision the young man did see:
A lad trying to run and jump into his trousers hung up on the branch of a tree. *Chorus*

'Allow me to show you a trick. Just step in with one leg at a time…'
The lad was so grateful he scarcely could speak and ran off in the blink of an eye.
'Since fools I have now counted three, I'll return to the first one of all.
O Lord there be so many fools in this world, it's a wonder it turns round at all.'

And it's Oh, such a silly, my word such a silly I never did see such a silly before,
But now I have found three other such sillies I've come back your daughter to wed.

♩.=91 — **A sect:**

The young man was come to woo 'Dear daughter go fetch some beer' No matter how long they did wait 'twas in vain The daughter did never appear The old woman she went down the stair 'Dear daughter, what ails you?' she said 'O Mother just see the great axe in the beam What if it should fall on my head?' And its

B sect:

O such a silly, my word such a silly, I never did see such a silly before If ever I find three such sillies again I'll come back your daughter to wed (The)

The Juggler

Say, have you seen the man with the hands,
Say, have you seen the hands of the juggler?
There are one, two, three, four balls in the air,
At any moment you will catch him...
Juggling with clubs and hats and staves,
With knives and plates and jacks and knaves.
Come, watch the juggler!

Say, have you seen the man with the feet,
Say, have you seen the feet of the juggler?
There are one, two, three, four balls in the air,
At any moment you will catch him...
Juggling with rods and golden rings,
With apples and pears and falcons' wings.
Come, watch the juggler!

Say, have you seen the man with the arms,
Say, have you seen the arms of the juggler?
There are one, two, three, four torches aflare,
At any moment you will catch him...
Juggling with impulse and desire,
With flaming frost and frozen fire.
Come, watch the juggler!

Say, have you seen the man with the eyes,
Say, have you seen the eyes of the juggler?
See him spinning round on the spot,
At any moment you will catch him...
Juggling with meteorites and things
And sun and moon and Saturn's rings.
Come, watch the juggler!

Say, have you seen the man with the face,
Say, have you seen the face of the juggler?
Hear the silence hum as he spins,
At any moment you will catch him...
Juggling with cup and sword and all,
While time and space in darkness fall.
Behold, the Juggler!

♩=149 **A sect:**

Say, have you seen the man with the hands Say, have you seen the hands of the jug-gler? There are one, two, three, four balls in the air At any mom-ent you will catch him... Jug-gling with

B sect:

clubs and hats and staves With knives and plates and jacks and knaves Come, watch the jug-gler (Say,)

Jehanne's effortlessly eloquent verses lift one's spirits with a power echoing that of John Clare, W. H. Davies, Robert Frost and R. S. Thomas. Nature gives birth to us, nurtures us and receives us back with a welcome embrace once our journey is complete. *Earth Songs* reflects that journey and it touched my soul, both by reminding me of my own connection to the glory of Mother Nature, growing up as a country boy in the beautiful Wye and Usk valleys in Wales, and by its link to my darling Polly and to the power of her desire, through Stop Ecocide, to protect and enhance the sanctity of nature and the very life it gives us.

Ian Lawrie KC, husband of Earth lawyer Polly Higgins

Afterword
Jojo Mehta

I have been asked many times what brought me to the co-founding of Stop Ecocide International with pioneering barrister Polly Higgins. It has become clear to me that the songs in this book were the beginning of that journey.

They were the deep thread of care for the Earth along which my childhood was strung, with bead-like moments: herb robert and deadnettle lining a path into sloping Oxfordshire fields, butterflies wing-shimmying on purple buddleia in summer, stick-writing in the wet sand of a Brittany beach, orchids and cowslips on Minchinhampton common, rough track undergrowth near Carcassonne under the moon, blackthorn in the Burleigh hedgerows, wallflowers against Cotswold stone…

That meandering thread would ultimately lead me to on-the-ground environmental activism, where I discovered a deep commitment, and a kindred spirit in Polly, whose gentle charisma and unquenchable determination still inspire so many. When I first joined her in the work toward recognition of ecocide as an international crime, I didn't expect to be co-founding a global campaign in support of ecocide law, still less inheriting it when Polly passed away in 2019.

Five years later here we are, with a presence in 50 countries. The EU has just criminalised conduct 'comparable to ecocide'. The conversation at the International Criminal Court is moving forward, led by the courage and determination of the Republic of Vanuatu in the South Pacific Ocean.

We fully expect that a proposal to amend the Rome Statute to add the crime of ecocide (alongside genocide, crimes against humanity, war crimes and the crime of aggression) will be forthcoming in the near future. The direction of travel is already clear: ecocide law will provide the legal guardrail to steer humanity toward safety, and into balance with the living world of which we are an inextricable part.

I believe it is a precious privilege to be alive, in this moment of crisis and awakening, as conscious physical beings, able to both experience and influence the unique, extraordinary living system that is Earth, our natural home. My mother's songs speak to the depth and wonder of this relationship: to the body, the rhythms and the spirit of it.

Also, like ecocide law, to the responsibility inherent in it.

May they continue to be sung.

Jehanne is truly a Bard: singer, songwriter and musician, a lyrically poetic Storyteller of our Time and of Times to Come. As well as being a powerful speaker and vocalist, she has developed her own unique Way of Sound Healing. Jehanne's is the voice of a modern warrior: she awakens Listening. Words she has forged resound onwards in peoples' hearts and minds and deeds, calling each one of us to stand up and become Guardians of the Earth, our Home.

Christopher Bee, spiritual ecologist

Acknowledgements

This songbook sat in the realm of intention for a lot longer than I meant it to. But I have faith in the weavings of life and time, and conclude that the book is emerging exactly when it should, as both legacy and seed for the future; as a recognition and a passing forward of Jehanne's life-work; as well as a material support for the advocacy toward legal protection for the Earth.

Huge thanks go to Stu McLellan for his sensitive visual interpretations that complement the songs so well and make the pages such a joy to turn; to transcriber Aeron Z Jones and proofreaders Thol Mason and Matt Wimpress who skilfully made the melodies and chords available for anyone to sing; to Jonathon Porritt for his foreword, his staunch support and a lifetime of dedication to protecting the Earth; to Adrian and Gracie and Graham at Little Toller for trusting in the project and for designing and producing the book so beautifully.

Of course, to my mother Jehanne for the songs themselves; and to my father Rob for always being there, with her and for her, in music and in life.

Thanks also to all those who have supported this publication. By doing so you have supported these songs to make their way in the world, and you have also supported the work of Stop Ecocide International, which is the beneficiary of all royalties from the book.

Amy Aldington
Angela Findlay
Angie Burke
Aonghus Gordon OBE
Arthur Mehta
Beatrice Hook
Bianca Pitt, SHE Changes Climate
Caba family & FitzRoy family
Chloe Goodchild
Chris Leslie
Christer Soderberg, CircleCarbon.com
Christopher Bee, GerhardReisch.com

Claudia Scholler Cortijo Saltador
David Morrison
Elaine Vijaya Nash & Fred Hageneder
Elisabeth Bamford
Emma Winkley & Andy Kane
Esmeralda de Belgique
Frederic Brehmer
Gabriella Songbird Kapfer, Resounding Earth
Gatekeeper Trust
Grace Trevett
Graham Kennish
H. Pennig

[continued overleaf]

Heather Stewart Dorrell
Helen Chadwick
Ian Lawrie KC
James D'Angelo
Jan Allen
Jeannine Bednar-Giyose
Jo Little
John & Gillian
John Barker & Michael Mehta
Jonathan Durham
Kamala Raymakers
Kate Mackintosh
Kelvin Hall
Laurie McNeill
Lot Locher
Louise Sinclair
Lyndon DeVantier
Margaretha Johanna Wewerinke-Singh
Mark Mathews
Martin Palmer
Matthew Shribman
Missy Lahren
Monica Lennon, Member of the Scottish Parliament

Neesa Copple
Paul Goodenough
Pella Thiel
Peter & Sarah Dawkins
Polly Henderson
Rob de Laet
Robin Cooper
Rosa Julia Davis
Sally & Shay Cleaver
Sarah Windrum
Sheri Sophia Herndon
Sylvia Ezen
Tamzin Titford-Mock
Thomas Gooch
Thomas Jones
Tony & Sue Matthews
TraceyKay Coe
Vanya Orr
Georgia Taylor, Wealden Green Party
Wiene Locher
Will Lawrence
Yew Tree Press of Stroud
Zambodhi Hill

Our Mother
Jehanne Mehta

Our mother
You who are the
deep temple
of the living Earth

The song of Your sacred name
resounds
in the shimmering pathways
of our resurrecting bodies

Your realm of
nurturing warmth and abundance
is the womb
from which we awaken
into our true being

From the core of Your
glimmering darkness
Your ever constant intent is
the birth of love
flooding all creation
from within

We receive with gratitude each day
the selfless outpouring
of Your being

Your radiant presence
empowers our loving forgiveness
that we may honour and respect
our earthly vessels as the
shining temples they truly are

We commit ourselves
in reverence and love
to Your cycles of living and dying
unfolding and releasing

Within Your loving being
is born the power of the human I
to direct all that is astray
into its place of healing

For You
our Mother
Are the soil of our growth and becoming
the portal and the power of our birthing
and within the ever renewing glory of Your love
shines
the circle
of our freedom

                                              It is so

While this is her first songbook, Jehanne's poetry is published in a number of books and anthologies. Her rendering of a prayer to the universal mother is included here to give a sense of the deep spirit of the feminine that animates all of Jehanne's work, and of the dauntless reverence with which she approaches both life and writing.

www.jehannemehta.com
www.stopecocide.earth
www.littletoller.co.uk